FINDING THE TREASURE

FINDING THE TREASURE

GOOD NEWS FROM THE ESTATES

Reflections from the Church of England
Estates Theology Project

EDITED BY AL BARRETT

First published in Great Britain in 2023

SPCK
36 Causton Street
London SW1P 4ST
www.spck.org.uk

British Library Cataloguing-in-Publication Data
A catalogue record for this book is available from the British Library

ISBN 978-0-281-08805-8

eBook ISBN 978-0-281-08806-5

1 3 5 7 9 10 8 6 4 2

Typeset by Fakenham Prepress Solutions, Fakenham, Norfolk NR21 8NL

First printed in Great Britain by Clays Limited

eBook by Fakenham Prepress Solutions, Fakenham, Norfolk NR21 8NL

Produced on paper from sustainable sources

Contents

For the faith-full people of our estate churches and parishes, and their everyday witness to God's treasure in their lives and their neighbourhoods

Foreword

ANN MORISY

It may be apocryphal, but it was said that the courage that informed the writers of *Faith in the City* was rooted in a disclosure by the Methodist Church about its response to anxiety about future viability. It had made a conscious decision to invest in the most successful suburban churches, only to realise later that the loss of a footing in poor communities could never be restored. They beseeched the Church of England not to make the same error. There are echoes here of the situation which the Church now faces in relation to estate-based ministry.

Rumour has it that I initiated the first estate-based ministry forum way back in 1990 when I was Community Ministry Adviser for London Diocese. I identified deeply with those ministering in the neglected and unloved estates north of the Thames, especially as so often they were surrounded by so many glamorous and upmarket parishes. There must have been times when they wondered why they had been condemned to such weary-making and disregarded ministry, and I think I identified with this too. Despite this unpromising foundation, together we sensed signs of blessing in generous amounts. Unfortunately, the wider church, and the wider polity, both continue in their failure to see and value such precious and sustaining glimpses of humanity. As Bishop Philip North rightly says, the pearl that seems so precious to us seems unimportant to others.

This book, with its compilation of stories and theological reflections, uncovers the positives that a local church fosters when it engages with its neighbourhood. Social geographers have known this for some time, so too those concerned with urban regeneration

– it is indeed good to welcome theologians to the party. However, this book also chastises the wider church, sometimes forcefully, for squandering the community benefit of outward facing churches. This lack of imagination, or lack of interest, will result in church leaders ceding their right to speak publicly about poverty and the precariousness of life for so many in this country. If ministry on estates is allowed to wither, then the commentary of our church leaders on government policy in relation to deprivation and injustice will be mocked for its hypocrisy and naïveté.

The methodology displayed in this book provides a template for future theological reflection and commentary. It provides a lens through which to give value to the often unnoticed and undervalued outcomes that flow when the church engages with seemingly unloved places. Today I find myself living in a particularly unloved place, a place where the majority of residents have been forgotten, except by the exceptional people who are prepared to care for us. I am grateful for an insight from David Ford, as I contemplate the rest of my life living with the restrictions of paralysis. He writes of how in our lives, we may be faced with *multiple overwhelmings*. And now this is my experience. I hope it is not presumptuous to claim solidarity with the many residents of housing estates who likewise experience multiple overwhelming – whether through disappointment, lack, humiliation, addiction, and much more besides. Labouring under the impact of these emotional and sometimes physical assaults can bring scarring that impedes both personal and communal flourishing, but this does not have to be the case.

In May 2022, I faced the most significant overwhelming of my life. I broke my neck in an accident on a day out at a theme park. Despite the best efforts of surgeons and therapists, I remain paralysed from the shoulders down. I have indeed endured multiple overwhelmings. The challenges have been intense, and no doubt will continue to be for the rest of my life. And what about faith? I can boast of having only a hesitant faith (although a great fan of Jesus!). However, with profound sincerity, I declare that even this flimsy faith has been sufficient. My modest faith has sustained me in a way that I could not have dared hope for, and thanks be to

God for this. Please may those who minister on Britain's housing estates, and those who reflect on that ministry, never forget that it is the encouragement of faith, however hesitant, that is the greatest gift to those who grapple with multiple overwhelmings.

Ann Morisy

Contexts and contributors

The Revd Dr Al Barrett

Revd Dr Al Barrett has been Rector of Hodge Hill (in east Birmingham) since 2010, and since then has been engaged in a long-term, intergenerational journey of community-building with his neighbours on the Firs and Bromford estate. Al's PhD research, emerging from his practice locally, was published as *Interrupting the Church's Flow: A Radically Receptive Political Theology in the Urban Margins*,[1] and he is also co-author (with Ruth Harley) of *Being Interrupted: Reimagining the Church's Mission from the Outside, In*.[2] Al has been convenor of the Church of England Estates Theology Project since its inception in 2017, and continues to research, write and convene reflective learning spaces around questions of missiology, community, politics, ecology and spirituality, with a recent focus on critical theologies of masculinity and whiteness.

Bishop Philip North

Philip North is currently the suffragan Bishop of Burnley in the Diocese of Blackburn, and later this year will become the tenth Bishop of Blackburn. He began ministry in the Diocese of Durham, serving outer estates parishes in Sunderland and Hartlepool, and then spent six years ministering to pilgrims to the Shrine of Our Lady of Walsingham as Priest Administrator. He then returned to parochial ministry as Team Rector of the Parish of Old St Pancras, serving a large area of North West London around Camden Town, and was consecrated Bishop and moved to Lancashire in February 2015. He has a strong interest in issues around poverty and social justice and in the vitality of the urban church, and is a member of Church of England's Renewal and Reform Estates Evangelism

Task Group. He is a member of the Company of Mission Priests, a dispersed community who live to a rule in order to focus their lives on the mission of the church, especially among the poor.

Wythenshawe (team ministry), Manchester

The Revd Canon Dr Stephen Edwards

Stephen Edwards is Vice-Dean of Worcester Cathedral and was previously Team Rector of Wythenshawe in the Diocese of Manchester. The Wythenshawe Team, one of the largest in the Church of England, covers an area to the north of Manchester Airport and began its life between the World Wars as an overspill estate built on garden city principles. Before serving in Wythenshawe, Stephen was Rector of St Agnes' Longsight, an inner-city parish in Manchester, which provided the foundation of his doctoral research about being a White male priest in a majority Black congregation. Before that he served in parishes in Colwyn Bay after being ordained in the Church in Wales.

The Revd Canon Dr James Hawkey

James Hawkey is Canon Theologian of Westminster Abbey, Visiting Professor in Theology at King's College London and a Bye-Fellow of Clare College, Cambridge. He served his curacy at St Mary's Church in inner-city Portsmouth, and for much of this project was Dean of Clare College, Cambridge, working alongside Stephen Edwards in Wythenshawe. He is a member of The Faith and Order Commission of the Church of England, and a Chaplain to HM The King.

Rubery (St Chad's), Birmingham

The Revd Claire Turner

Claire Turner is a Parish Priest who, having served her curacy in Wednesfield, an urban parish in North East Wolverhampton, is currently the Vicar of St Chad's Church in Rubery. Sitting on the edge of Birmingham Diocese, Rubery consists of both outer estate neighbourhoods and those that look more toward the open spaces of Worcestershire's Waseley Hills. She undertook her ministerial training at The Queen's Foundation for Ecumenical Theological Education, Birmingham, where, in 2012, she successfully completed her MA thesis. Claire's postgraduate study built on her background in the arts, most notably her role as Curator of Education and Interpretation at internationally renowned contemporary art space, Ikon Gallery in Birmingham. Here, she produced a wide range of resources and projects designed to provide visitors with a platform on which to build and articulate meaning, a task that continues to inform her priestly ministry. She is currently engaged in PhD research which she hopes will result in a thesis entitled 'Curatorial Practice as a Model to Support the Development of Hermeneutical Competence amongst Christian Congregations'.

With thanks also for support from:
Dr Ashley Cocksworth (Tutor, The Queen's Foundation, Birmingham)
Professor Anthony Reddie (Oxford Centre for Religion and Culture)

Eltham, South London

Nick Russell CA

Nick Russell is a Church Army Lead Evangelist with a psychology background who has been living in various deprived estates in South East London since 1999. He manages a children's and families' charity that specializes in working with youth drug gang members, and which employs local workers with lived experience of poverty, violence, drugs and crime. He is also responsible for looking after his local church and developing fresh expressions of church there.

The Revd Dr Carlton Turner

Carlton Turner is a contextual and practical theologian and Anglican Tutor at The Queen's Foundation for Ecumenical Theological Education, Birmingham. Before teaching theology, Carlton spent eight years as incumbent on a Black Country outer urban estate in the Diocese of Lichfield. His PhD into the intersections of church and culture in a post-slavery, post-colonial African Caribbean context has sharpened his attention to culture and context, particularly when it comes to ministry in diverse and deprived settings. Besides teaching Mission and Theological Reflection for Ordinands and Readers going on placements, Carlton continues to research the realities of ministry within the Church of England, notably UKME (United Kingdom Minority Ethnic) and Global Majority Heritage experiences and ministry among the laity.

Twydall (Holy Trinity), Gillingham, Kent

The Revd Ann Richardson

Ann Richardson is the Area Dean of Aston and Sutton Coldfield in Birmingham Diocese. While *Finding the Treasure* was being conceived, she was the Vicar of Holy Trinity, Twydall, on the edge of Gillingham, Kent. Having grown up in Thamesmead in South-East London, the riches and challenges of estate life are a formational part of her own character and story.

Dr Justin Stratis

Justin Stratis is Professor of Systematic Theology at Wycliffe College, University of Toronto. Prior to this he was, for nine years, Tutor in Christian Doctrine at Trinity College, Bristol, where he trained students for vocational ministry in the Church of England and other Christian denominations. During his time in England, he became convinced of the detrimental effects of class discrimination in the church and British society in general. His participation in the Estates Theology Project afforded him the chance to shine a spotlight on the crucial contribution of the working classes in church flourishing. It is his conviction that the health of the church depends upon those with historic privilege letting go of power and giving way to those on the margins to lead and educate the body of Christ.

Durrington (St Symphorian), Worthing, West Sussex

The Revd Ben Eadon

Ben Eadon is Vicar of the parishes of St Bartholomew's and St Paul's in Brighton. Before that he was Vicar of St Symphorian's, Durrington. He was in post in Durrington while working on this project. He is also a member of the Company of Mission Priests, a dispersed congregation of priests in the Church of England under the patronage of St Vincent de Paul and St Matthew which is committed to serving in places of challenge and deprivation.

With thanks also to **Dr Elizabeth Powell** (Cambridge University)

Our grateful thanks go also to other travelling-companions who have participated in and supported the project along the way:
Cowgate, Newcastle: Revd Alan Paterson and Dr Anna Rowlands (Durham University)
Dr Nigel Rooms (Church Mission Society)
Dr Andrew Grinnell (Poverty Truth Network)
Revd Dr Genny Tunbridge (Common Ground Community, Hodge Hill)
Sam Richardson and Alison Barr (SPCK)
Revd Canon Abi Thompson (Sub-Dean, St Alban's Cathedral)
Dave Champness (EETG)
Simon Jarvis (Whistledown Productions)
Tashi Lasalle (Church of England, Communications)

Introduction

BISHOP PHILIP NORTH

The story behind this project is twofold. The first is a bold and ambitious gospel vision endorsed unanimously by the General Synod of the Church of England. The second was a short and intense row in a comfortable sitting room in a Cambridge College.

The ambitious vision is the renewal of church life on the urban estates of our nation, necessary because we face a crisis in the urban church. In 2015, the Church Commissioners released data demonstrating that we invest £5 per head on ministry to urban estates, way below the national average of £9 per head. The impact of this sustained under-investment on the ground is plain to see. Estates churches are small, and they are getting smaller at an alarming speed. Congregational size on estates is 0.8 per cent of the population compared to 1.7 per cent nationally. The rate of congregational decline in estates churches is four times the national average. Forty per cent of applications for church building closures are in the 10 per cent most deprived communities. For the past 30 years we have seen the slow erosion of Christian presence on our urban estates as buildings are closed down, stipendiary posts are withdrawn and parishes are merged. In 20 years' time, the presence of the established church on the nation's urban estates could be no more than a memory.

All of this creates a critical evangelistic problem. The ministry of Jesus Christ was powerfully focused on the margins. He called the poor to be his followers. He placed the forgotten at the centre of the community. He held up as examples of kingdom living the unvoiced – children, the disabled, peasant women, sinners,

The ministry of Jesus Christ was powerfully focused on the margins.

1

Gentiles. And from those beginnings he brought about a kingdom movement that utterly transformed what it means to be human.

Consequently, all fruitful renewal movements in the church have very swiftly heard a call to serve the poor. Whether it be the early church and its care for slaves and widows, St Francis placing himself with the lepers, Vincent de Paul reaching out to galley slaves and prisoners, John Wesley preaching the gospel outdoors to the rural poor or the Oxford Movement planting churches into the great urban slums, the gospel makes a difference when it is lived out among the forgotten and the marginalized.

And yet the Church of England appears to be implementing a policy that does the complete reverse. We appear to seek renewal by abandoning precisely those areas from which renewal has always come. A church that leaves behind the poor may make sense to the accountants, but it will no longer be the body of Christ. Reversing the decline of Christian presence on our urban estates must therefore be a critical priority.

The Estates Evangelism Task Group was formed as part of the Church of England's Renewal and Reform programme in 2016 in order to address this issue. Its guiding vision is a very simple one – to have a loving, serving, worshipping Christian community on every significant urban estate in the country. There is evidence that some dioceses are responding to this challenge, with a large number of precious new churches starting up in estates across the country and greater support for existing estates churches.

But while the vision is straightforward one, the challenges are vast. These are in part around resources. Many Church of England dioceses are financially stretched and can ill-afford to invest in estates churches that are never likely to be viable financially. We are living with a shortage of vocations, which means that priests willing to work on estates can be hard to find. Moreover, a disproportionate amount of the church's historic wealth is held by a small number of southern dioceses, and there is little sign that they are willing to redistribute any of it to poorer areas.

Even greater are the evangelistic challenges. When I visit a new church, I can almost always guess the congregational size based on the deprivation levels of the community that it serves. In areas that have been reduced to dependency by years of austerity and cutbacks, where leaders are hard to form, where local people feel a frustration with institutions that have proven untrustworthy, where worship can seem arcane and irrelevant and where hope can be hard to find, sustaining recognizable patterns of Christian life is an awesome task.

But all the issues and problems that afflict the church are at heart theological. Surely the main reason that we are struggling to sustain viable estates churches is that we seem to be getting our gospel proclamation wrong. No one wants to listen to us. The pearl that seems so precious to us seems unimportant to others. We struggle to communicate the life and person of Jesus Christ in a way that connects with people's lives. Many may want to point out that this is a national problem that afflicts the whole church, and the same complaint is made by those who work with young people, or students, or those in wealthier areas. But it seems heightened on estates, which is why this area of work matters so much. Cultural transfer almost always goes from poor to rich. If we can get our evangelistic approaches right on the estates, there will be learning that is applicable anywhere.

It is easy to identify the mistakes that churches make in evangelism to estates (especially easy for me because I have made most of them myself). Some churches emphasize a gospel of unconditional love which they express through generous and often heroic service, drawing alongside the poor and meeting human needs. But they never quite get round to explaining why or inviting people into life-giving relationship with Jesus Christ. Other churches will emphasize a message of sin and forgiveness, but they struggle to be heard by people who feel (and indeed perhaps are) more sinned against than sinning. If we are serious about renewing church life on our urban estates, we need to think hard about the way we communicate the gospel. Sustainable estates evangelism requires a refreshed theology.

And this is where the short and intense row comes into play. For many years I have had concerns about the growing disparity between the world of the church and that of academic theology. Aware of the priority of evangelism in a secular age and yearning for simple messages, the church can often seem dismissive of its theologians. At the same time, theologians often appear uninterested in the needs of the church and the mission field and address instead questions that are set for them by fellow academics or their own middle-class social networks. Over the years, I have made numerous attempts to bring these two worlds more into dialogue but have struggled to find theologians who are really interested in engaging in depth with the local church in urban areas.

And so, sitting in his comfortable sitting room overlooking the quad at Clare College, I launched into a sustained broadside along these lines against the amiable and unsuspecting Dean, Dr James Hawkey. He was vigorous in response, and the conversation ended in a challenge. I would find six estates practitioners who were willing to do some in-depth thinking on the theology that lay behind their ministry. He would find six academic theologians who would draw alongside the practitioners over a period of two years, visit them in their parishes and engage deeply with estates residents.

We were both able to deliver, and so the work began. Our aim was to provide a theological engine room for the Estates Evangelism project.

The task was harder to define than we thought and has benefited enormously from the clear and challenging leadership of Dr Al Barrett, who has the advantage of being both an estates practitioner and an academic. The original question I posed was, 'What is the good news for the estates?' My thinking was that, through a process of listening, the group would be able to rethink how we present and communicate the gospel such that it connects with the lives of estates residents. I hoped that this would provide guidance and inspiration for estates church leaders and for resource providers and enable them to teach, preach and evangelize in ways that connect with the lives of estates people.

But where does the good news lie? Is it like property, exclusive to the church and something that we have the power to import from one place to another, stopping only to ensure that the language we use is making the desired impact? Or is the nature of Jesus' presence rather less definable? In the Parable of the Sheep and Goats in Matthew 25, Jesus is present in the hungry, the prisoner, the naked and the thirsty. In serving them, we serve him. He is not only proclaimed in the ministry of the church; he is also discovered. We don't need to carry Jesus from one place to another because he is already there!

So we began to see that our task was not to frame the good news for a different context. Much more challengingly, it was to seek the good news *together*. It was to be about patient and sustained listening to context with the aim of discovering the presence of Jesus in company. It was not about good news *for* the estates. What we sought was good news *from* the estates. In the words of one of the theologians, Justin Stratis, 'We go as beggars seeking bread.'

> **What we sought was good news *from* the estates. In the words of one of the theologians, Justin Stratis, 'We go as beggars seeking bread.'**

All too often as Christians we get our listening wrong. Either we simply fail to listen because we think we already know, or we listen cursorily in order to give ourselves an excuse to voice pre-formed answers. We hoped that the listening in this project would be different because we planned to start off with no idea where we would finish up. We simply trusted that along the way we would meet with Jesus, and that when we met him, we would worship him.

Inevitably, there have been developments as the project has progressed. Two theologians, sadly those most embedded in the academy, had to withdraw because the pressures of university life proved incompatible with participation in the project. Very movingly, one of our practitioners also pulled out, speaking openly about the ways in which working on an estate that was lacking confidence had undermined his own confidence. That in itself made a point to the wider group about the level of the challenge that estates church leaders face.

There have been other voices that have challenged the need for the project itself. 'Why bother with all that theology? Just get on with the job!' one bishop said to me at a meeting. But my contention is that, without this patient listening, the rest of the work would simply collapse. Any work of mission must begin with God. If it doesn't, it will come to nothing.

And throughout the work, we have been fed by the stories. The schoolchild who named meeting her theologian as the best thing that had ever happened to her. The members of the public who could open up about their lives and the role of the church while weaving. The opportunities people have found to express themselves, to name issues and to build relationships. The imagination of our practitioners and the generosity of the theologians. And always in the midst of it all, the treasure we seek and for which we would sacrifice everything, Jesus, wonderfully present.

We hope that you learn something from the theological reflections and experiences of ministry that are contained in this book. But above all we hope that you learn from our method. Listen deeply to the communities you serve, and do so above all through simple one-to-one conversation. Ask what gives people joy and what gives them grief. Give them time to talk about themselves, even if what you hear seems mundane and unexciting. And listen with an open heart, not thinking you know the answers, resisting those simplistic solutions to complex questions that so easily form on the Christian tongue. Just listen, and you will find the treasure.

1

Finding the treasure: Rooting our reflections

AL BARRETT

A parable from the estate

With what can we compare the kingdom of God, or what parable will we use for it?
(Mark 4.30)

Well, how about a tapestry of many different coloured threads, woven together by many different hands? That image, from Wythenshawe, Manchester, is just one of many 'parables of the kin-dom'[1] we'll discover through the pages of this book, through the stories of, and reflections on, adventures of deep listening among church communities and wider neighbourhoods in five estate parishes across England.

A number of different interweavings can be traced through this book. The first, as seen clearly with the Wythenshawe Weave, is the interweaving of the lives and stories of *church members and their neighbours*, making the complex tapestries that those of us who are Anglican might often name 'the parish'.

In a second dimension of this tapestry, those everyday and miraculous stories of life in a place are interwoven with *God's Story*, as we encounter it primarily in Scripture. This is no simple (local) question and (biblical) answer, but again, a complex interweaving that we might describe as 'discovering the good news together'.

Third, we might imagine the multicoloured threads from one particular local church community's journey, interweaving with those from other churches in other places, together making up 'Church' (with a capital C), *the body of Christ* that stretches across time and space. In *this* dimension of the tapestry (as much if not more than in any of the others), we might be sharply aware that some threads tend to be overlooked or even discarded. Some are so delicate that they are getting increasingly frayed and close to breaking point (the phrase 'hanging on by a thread' says a lot). Conversely, some contributions to this tapestry might be so thick and heavy that they risk dominating the picture, displacing the more fragile to the peripheries, making any kind of interweaving (with its relationships of complex interdependence) near impossible.

This book, then, is a weaving together of threads from five different contexts, where church and neighbourhood have already interwoven; and of experiences, stories and reflections from local residents, locally rooted practitioners of ministry, and academic theologians with roots in other places and institutions. No single agenda unites the threads presented here (and at times that will, no doubt, make for an awkward sense of unevenness) – other than, that is, the deep desire to pay careful, discerning attention to any emerging patterns in what God is weaving among us, in and through our estate communities.

Finding

The kingdom of heaven is like treasure hidden in a field, which someone found and hid; then in his joy he goes and sells all that he has and buys that field.
(Matthew 13.44)

Or what woman having ten silver coins, if she loses one of them, does not light a lamp, sweep the house, and search carefully until she finds it? When she has found it, she calls together her friends and neighbours, saying, 'Rejoice with me, for I have found the coin that I had lost.'
(Luke 15.8–9)

This book's title, *Finding the Treasure*, comes from Jesus' brief, one-verse parable in Matthew's Gospel. The content of this book is testimony to the kinds of 'kin-dom treasure' that its contributors have found in the estate contexts where they have spent time and given attention. This treasure has been found in the form of *loves* and *griefs*, in relationships of *kindness* and *care*, in places of *refuge* and *hope* (Wythenshawe). It has been encountered, in liminal spaces, as 'life, community, creativity, desire' (Rubery). It has been experienced as a *deep spirituality*, grounded in *generosity* and *compassion*, that transcends crude binaries (Eltham). It presents itself in bold *affirmations* and *rejections*, which present profound challenges to the wider church (Twydall). And it is unearthed as *resourcefulness*, *resilience* and a palpable sense of *beauty* in and around the apparently ordinary (Durrington).

There are at least two ways in which such treasure has been found. First, it has been stumbled upon. We turn the corner of a street, or cross the threshold of someone's home, or a conversation takes us on a twisting, turning journey – and suddenly the treasure is there, in front of us, staring us in the face. Is this how the 'treasure hidden in a field' is found? Someone is merely wandering through that field, glances down at their feet for a moment, and there it is, shining up at them? Requiring of them nothing more than an unintended detour, an unconscious turn of the head, and eyes at least half open to notice the unexpected.

The parable of the woman with the coins suggests a second way of finding – as the result of *careful searching*. This finding requires intentionality (method, even), thoroughness, perseverance and, most critically, sustained attention. This way, we will not find if we are not looking. We will not hear if we are not listening. We will not discover if we are not expectant – even if *what* we see or hear or discover is beyond any of our preconceptions or imaginings. Much of what we share in these pages is the fruit of such careful,

We will not discover if we are not expectant – even if *what* we see or hear or discover is beyond any of our preconceptions or imaginings.

9

sustained *treasure-seeking*. And that has been necessary because the kind of treasure we describe here has often been hidden – or even lost – to many of us.

Hiding

> He told them another parable: 'The kingdom of heaven is like yeast that a woman took and mixed in with [or hid within] three measures of flour until all of it was leavened.'
> (Matthew 13.33)

> It is like a mustard seed, which, when sown upon the ground, is the smallest of all the seeds on earth; yet when it is sown it grows up and becomes the greatest of all shrubs, and puts forth large branches, so that the birds of the air can make nests in its shade.
> (Mark 4.31–32; cf. Matthew 13.31–32)

The most obvious reason for hiding treasure is precisely so that it is *not* found. I might hide some treasure because it belongs to me and I want to 'save it for a rainy day' (whenever and whatever that 'rainy day' might be). I might also be hiding this treasure because I don't want anyone else to have it. The dominant mindset here is one of *possession*, *competition* and *anxiety*, driven by an assumption of *scarcity*: 'There is not enough to share freely, so I must keep this to myself, hidden away until I need it.' Or, alternatively, 'I have more than enough myself, but I don't like the idea of others having as much or more than me, so I will do everything I can to make sure they don't discover the treasure that I know is there for the finding.'

If there is treasure to be found in abundance in our estate communities if we only look for it, then in what sense is such treasure hidden, and why? One clue might be found in the governmental language of 'deprivation'. Many of our estate neighbourhoods rank among the highest in the country in indices of multiple deprivation (IMDs), which include factors related to income, employment, education, health, crime, barriers to housing and services, and 'living environment'. Labelling a neighbourhood as 'deprived' might well highlight some of the multiple pressures on the lives of local people; some of the barriers to people, relationships and communities flourishing; some of the inequalities between this area and other places.

But there are dangers within this language too. It defines places, and their people, only in terms of what they *lack*. It labels them as 'problems to be solved'. At worst, it implicitly suggests that their 'deprivation' is *something about them, their responsibility, their fault*. And it is hardly surprising that when such language is used repeatedly about a place and its people by those commentating from outside, then slowly and surely those on the inside begin to absorb it and believe it about themselves. How many funding bids require those of us who live and work in estate neighbourhoods to tell the most desperate story of lack and need we can summon up, in the hope that *our* need will be more persuasive to the funders than that of the neighbourhood down the road? It's little wonder, in such circumstances, that we're falling over ourselves to hide our treasure away.

An alternative way of describing neighbourhoods like ours is as places not of 'deprivation', but of 'suppressed abundance'. We may not be financially rich, we may have a history of being 'asset-stripped' by the forces of inequality and austerity, but there is an abundance of treasure here, if – as we have said already – we look carefully. And looking carefully often means looking *differently*: learning to *value* different kinds of 'treasure', making different decisions about 'what counts' and what is counted. 'Suppressed abundance' not only points us toward what is abundant, but also invites us to consider what – or who – is doing the *suppressing*. In whose interests is the real treasure of this neighbourhood being hidden? Who benefits from this neighbourhood believing that it counts for little? When some people are labelled as 'hard to reach', who is finding it hard to reach them? And if some are discounted as 'lost', then who has done the losing?

Jesus' parables of the kin-dom prompt us to ask such questions. But they also suggest strongly that the hiddenness of the kin-dom

When some people are labelled as 'hard to reach', who is finding it hard to reach them? is an inextricable aspect of how it comes to presence, life and growth within the world as we know it. Those who find themselves 'hidden' and 'overlooked' in our world – those discounted as 'little' or 'weak' or 'foolish' – turn out to be those who know most about what the kin-dom of God feels like and how it works. The kin-dom, glimpsed in Jesus' parables, subverts our understandings of value, worth and power.

And so the kin-dom is like a baker-woman (God?) who hides the leavening agent inside the dough in a way that dough and leaven become inseparable (interwoven, we might say, such that the binary of 'inside–outside' becomes meaningless) and – depending on your theology of leavened bread[2] – either contaminates the whole or brings the whole to a beautiful risen life. And the kin-dom is like tiny mustard seeds that literally sow themselves *everywhere* and – depending on your theology of gardening – either spread like the ugly, rampant weeds they are,[3] or bring their healing to edge-places disrupted by human carelessness, restoring habitats for a diverse multitude of species.[4] The hiddenness of the kin-dom is, at this level, a tactic of divine resistance: slipping through the fingers of those with institutional power and status, with their urges to 'manage' and control, uproot and discard – power games that residents of estate neighbourhoods have all too often found themselves on the receiving end of.

Responding

The New Testament is also clear, however, that it is *discovery*, and not hiddenness, that has the last word: everything that has been kept secret will be brought to light (Mark 4.22), and those who have been overlooked will be revealed in their glory as God's children (Rom. 8.19). At the heart of 'proclaiming the kingdom of God', the first of the Five Marks of Mission,[5] is exactly this: *discovering* where the kin-dom of God is 'close at hand', and *pointing* to it in ways that enable others to see it too. 'Discovering the good news together', as we have put it, involves processes of 'making the invisible, visible':[6] to neighbours, to local church members, to the wider church.

Jesus' parables of the kin-dom invite – and often describe within them – an active response to what has been discovered. Those parables we have touched on here beckon us into a (serious) game of hide and seek: there may be a tactical necessity in the divine treasure-*hiding*, but there is also often an eruption of joy and celebration in the treasure-*finding*. It is not surprising, for those of us who live in estate communities, that the finding of treasure is often accompanied, in Jesus' stories, by a gathering together of friends and neighbours for a riotous, all-night party. These are foretastes of the kin-dom that will be familiar to many of us! To accept such invitations, to be a guest and recipient of our neighbours' overflowing generosity and hospitality, to 'taste and see' that their freshly baked cakes are indeed full of the Lord's goodness: these are the kinds of responses that Christian disciples and ministers on estates are often called to – and what a joy and a privilege!

But to return, finally, to our opening parable – the treasure hidden in the field – we might well ask why the finder is compelled to 'sell all [s]he has' to buy the whole field, rather than, as perhaps we might be tempted to do, just taking it away with him when [s]he first discovers it?

It may depend, of course, on what kind of treasure our finder has found. A small box of gold trinkets would be all too easy to pocket and carry off. But what if the treasure, like the yeast or the mustard seed, takes a more organic form? What if its hiddenness is indeed because it has self-seeded and put down its roots right across the field, far too extensive to dig up and transplant, such that the only way to enjoy this treasure is to make your home *where the treasure is*. To give up all you previously counted as 'wealth' and make this place yours (alongside the birds of the air and all kinds of other unlikely kin who also count it as theirs). After all, as Jesus reminds us, 'where your treasure is, there your heart will be also' (Matt. 6.21).

Selling all we have and buying the whole field: there's the challenge for the church. Not simply 'throwing money' at estate communities

The much more profound challenge . . . is to recognize that the kinds of treasure we have both stumbled upon and actively sought out in these estate communities are gifts to be received, delighted in and celebrated.

from a detached distance (although for areas with long histories of systemic underinvestment and asset-stripping, getting their fair share of the common wealth should definitely be part of the picture). The much more profound challenge, brought to its focus in the Twydall Declaration that ends this book, is to recognize that the kinds of treasure we have both stumbled upon and actively sought out in these estate communities are gifts to be received, delighted in and celebrated, not just locally, by the churches in these places, but by the *whole* body of Christ.

'The Church of England *needs* Holy Trinity Twydall, in ways that a worldly perspective may not make entirely evident', write Justin Stratis and Ann Richardson in their chapter – just as the Church of England needs the people of Wythenshawe, Rubery, Eltham and Durrington too, and hundreds of other estate communities all over the country. We need the wonderful, surprising, abundant treasure that is deeply rooted in these places, not as something to extract for our own institutional survival, but because it is in these places that we will catch glimpses of the kin-dom of God springing up, growing and flourishing. It is in these places that – if we dare to let go of all we have counted as 'wealth' and make them our home, put down our roots and make it our mission to pay deep, sustained, loving attention to our neighbours and neighbourhoods – we will find ourselves, again and again, invited as guest, neighbour and friend to the kind of wild, celebratory parties that look, sound, smell, taste and feel just like the kin-dom of God.

2

Wythenshawe: The Garden City of God

STEPHEN EDWARDS AND JAMES HAWKEY

Setting the scene

Weaving in and out of seemingly endless rows of houses, the pathways and roadways of the Wythenshawe estate are typical of a garden city development planned before mass car ownership. On foot or by bicycle it is possible to deftly negotiate the complex patterns of roads and cul-de-sacs which seem otherwise designed to puzzle and disorientate the new arrival. The repeated housing units – solidly built and with great practicality and presence – were as confusing at the end of seven years of ministry on the estate as Stephen's first few weeks when he walked and walked to make sense of this sometimes infamous place.

Stephen knew about Wythenshawe before he arrived. But what he knew was only the twin 'givenness' of physical reality and the stubborn perception of the place from those outside. One of these 'givens' is easily attested to; the other is a myth bordering on slander. It is true that Wythenshawe has seen difficult times, has been paraded as a bad example, continues to suffer from significant and crippling levels of poverty, and through media representations as diverse as the backdrop for David Cameron's 'hug a hoodie' quip in 2006 or the Duchess of York's cringing 2009 documentary *The Duchess on the Estate*, Wythenshawe has had more than its fair share of attention.

A massive garden city estate, Wythenshawe's history is a chequered one, from its conception in the 1920s, followed by massive post-war growth, through difficult years of decline, unemployment and alienation, to its current revival brought about through significant investment, the Metrolink tram and its proximity to the Airport City investment. Wythenshawe has a population of between 70,000 and 110,000. The range in these numbers is not owing to transiency (the population of Wythenshawe is culturally static), but rather depends on how the area is defined. Manchester City Council's definition of the Wythenshawe wards is not always shared by the residents of the outer areas who still think of themselves as north Cheshire – a hundred years after being transferred. Local identity is fiercely proud of the neighbourhoods that comprise this vast community. It is a town but not a town, Manc but not Manchester, an estate and yet a garden city.

In and out of these given facts and myths – the reality and the ingrained perceptions of this place – the people of Wythenshawe weave their lives with resilience, determination and pride. For some, the seemingly constant external jibes and pressures of significant poverty have hardened lives to a core survival. For others, the crucible of this estate and its history and culture have nurtured creative, resilient and exemplary lives of service and hope.

The Church of England shares this unsettled history – as indeed do most of the remaining denominations on the estate. As the different building phases of the estate developed, so incredible church buildings were erected with iconic architecture, bold confidence and almost brash optimism. The Anglican churches are among the most important modernist structures in Manchester, and although one has closed for worship and another is currently not in use, these buildings are as much part of the social history as they are part of the built landscape.

The Wythenshawe Anglican Team ministry was one of the first in Manchester Diocese and one of the largest with a Team Rector, three Team Vicars, five churches and a cure of nearly 70,000 souls. However, despite their impressive architecture and impressive structural set-up, the churches in Wythenshawe all face acute difficulties of numbers, finance and capacity.

The congregations for the Wythenshawe churches are small, and this smallness is emphasized somewhat by the scale of the buildings in which they gather for worship. Built in 1965, William Temple Parish Church, designed by George Pace, is a tour de force of modernist confidence. Built to house 550 worshippers, its Lancashire steel girders, concrete and brick design was described by the architect as a 'workshop for worship'. Other churches within the Team are not quite so large, but have a similar story to tell: small congregations gather in buildings designed for a different era and, never full, are constant reminders of a bygone churchgoing age. Add into this mix the inevitable effects of age on post-war buildings, and the worshipping community often gathers in spite of the desperate state of these still-amazing buildings.

Just as the given parameters of Wythenshawe as a place (both in physical space and people's perception) are the framework through which the people weave their lives, so too with the churches: the backdrop of the physical plant and the given problems of a struggling system become the frame on which is woven a vibrant, colourful and often radical tapestry of Christian witness. Despite what John Atherton calls 'the great double whammy' of both community and church marginalization,[1] the ministry of the churches of Wythenshawe continues to tick the five boxes of mission creatively and naturally.[2] But this ministerial presence is fragile. The lack of long-term financial support is a constant weariness to those who, through their passion, compassion and faith, keep this work going. It is not unknown for projects – nearly always around food, hospitality and companionship – to rely solely on one-off grant funding, which is usually identified and obtained by the quick-thinking and deft skill of one or two people. The matching of such grants by the churches themselves is impossibly difficult, though by the grace and mercy of God the miracles do happen.

Manchester's cotton and textile history is less visible in the landscape of Wythenshawe than in older parts of the city, where the mills still pepper the area. But this cultural memory is strong and important. At a quiet afternoon on the theme of vulnerability and resilience, a number of activities were planned between the times of silence and the talks. One of these activities was very popular: a small weave no larger than a postcard. Those present were given a cardboard loom with the warp threads already prepared, and through this the weaver threaded wools of various colours to create a small weave. Each weft contained prayerful, meditative silence to create a textured pattern as a reminder of the quiet day.

The nature of the warp and weft which combined to create a woven material reflects the ways in which our community brought together the givenness – the warp of the built environment and the ingrained perceptions of the place – with the creative inter-action of the weft – the ebb and flow of life, working itself around the environment, creating vitality and enrichment. The weave of Wythenshawe life, like that of most communities, is an inter-action of the needs and desires of life with those things we come up against: obstacles that can block us and cause us to stumble, or, if negotiated deftly, can strengthen and define us.

The weave of Wythenshawe life . . . is an interaction of the needs and desires of life with those things we come up against: obstacles that can block us and cause us to stumble, or, if negotiated deftly, can strengthen and define us.

What was initially intended as a short activity for one afternoon became much more. Those present went home and spent a lot of time and care completing their mini weaves. The pride contained within them was not simply of a created piece, but of a shared journey with intentional prayers, reflections, hopes and dreams.

What if the weave was not just the work of one person, but of a larger community? And the prayers, hopes, dreams and fears not just individual intentions and concerns but a way of bringing together a wide group of people? What might that mean theologically, and what might it tell us about the church's vocation? Thus the Wythenshawe Weave project was born, and work started, involving as many people as we could. Armed with an extra-large frame, we took our loom to all the local churches and then right into the heart of the town centre, inviting anyone who wanted to weave their story, their hopes and their fears into the Wythenshawe Weave.

A theological approach

Many writers and preachers have observed that the biblical story of salvation begins in a garden and ends in a city. The narrative of Scripture unfolds from Eden, with all its creative potential, its bliss and its fruitfulness, and ultimately rests in a vision of the New Jerusalem. It's a vision, but not a fantasy. John the Divine, the traditional author of the book of Revelation, is a visionary, not a dreamer. This new city has highly distinctive features – its gates lie open continually, shut neither by day nor by night; it needs no source of light, other than the Lamb. But it retains some horticultural features, not least the trees either side of the river of the water of life, which have medicinal leaves, promised for the healing of the nations. From Genesis to Revelation, we read a story of God's faithfulness woven through the visceral drama of human history, which finds its ultimate truth and destiny in the call of Christ and his promise of new creation to a world fallen and devastatingly turned in upon itself.

Our work alongside the people of Wythenshawe's garden city was extremely conscious of narrative, of how individual stories relate to wider family and friendship groups, of how local experience enlarges, critiques and contradicts national policy and of how the message of the gospel both emerges from and connects with day-to-day life in a parish. The business of transformation is a complex one. The strong Christian tradition of *metanoia* (turning), prompted by Christian proclamation or preaching, is but one element in the ecosystem of Christian mission. Equally important is the rich Anglican tradition of presence and engagement, often signified by long-term commitment, faithful prayer and the patient nurturing of Christian community.

In his famous work, *Christianity and Social Order*, William Temple argued that it is the church's duty to announce Christian principles and to pass on to Christian citizens the task of reshaping social order. Christians have a distinctive responsibility to act as agents of transformation, pursuing freedom, fellowship and service, 'the three principles of a Christian social order, derived from the still more fundamental Christian postulates that man is a child of God and is destined for a life of eternal fellowship with him'.[3] This rich and challenging vision of Christian vocation has inspired generations to work faithfully alongside their non-Christian neighbours, in cultures that may seem far removed from the church, to pursue the common good and the dignity of all human beings.

The Wythenshawe project celebrated such a vision while developing a slightly sharper focus on pneumatology and culture.

The 'ordinariness' of culture is already an arena where the Holy Spirit is at work, and where the risen Christ awaits us in one another.

The 'ordinariness'[4] of culture is already an arena where the Holy Spirit is at work, and where the risen Christ awaits us in one another. In our Wythenshawe conversations it became clear how difficult it was to speak of any kind of straightforward binary between church and world in this context, any more than it is possible, standing in the great tradition of William Temple himself, to posit a strict dualism between 'sacred' and 'secular' forms of wisdom or truth. The relationship was always textured with multiple senses of belonging. Surely, we encountered wonderful individuals and families right at the heart of the church sharing the gospel and consciously working for mission in the wider culture. But it also became very clear that many of those touched by the work of the church were, formally speaking, very much on the fringes of day-to-day church life. More than this, as well as working with faithful members of the parish and ecumenical partners, our attention was intentionally focused on what went on beyond the church walls, set at a table in the middle of a shopping centre, asking questions about people's day-to-day experiences, and how the church might serve them better. 'Man,' argued Temple, 'is naturally and incurably social.'[5] Our work in Wythenshawe allowed us to encounter that 'social' reality on all sorts of levels, institutional, familial, in networks of work and friendship, with relationships that had been broken and relationships that were open to healing.

Temple wrote about *reshaping* the existing order so that it might better conform to Christian principles.[6] Christian engagement with wider society frequently relies on metaphors to describe that engagement. Having spent quite a lot of time listening to and working alongside residents, we decided on two of our own which developed and deepened as the project proceeded.

Our method was one of excavation and reweaving. This has been outlined before[7] as a kind of apostolic relationship, an exercise in the church's apostolicity which is focused on cultural transformation. In excavation, the church approaches the surrounding culture with care and respect, looking beneath the surface, paying close attention to context and integrity. Immersing itself in the wider culture, a local Christian community can come close to what makes that culture 'tick', and point toward what is already of Christ within it. This requires both humility and confidence: humility to recognize that creation itself is already a graced reality, and confidence in the gospel as a bottomless treasure for every place and every age. If excavation is to be taken seriously as a mode of Christian engagement, this requires patience and long-term commitment. Above all, such an approach is open to what the Holy Spirit is already doing within wider culture.

However, the demands of the gospel don't allow us just to leave it there. The church's primary vocation is, after all, to point to Christ and encourage others to follow him. Fortuitously, the Wythenshawe Weave project was beginning just as we were having conversations about theological method. The metaphor of reweaving arose quite naturally as a response both to the conversations we were having locally and out of a concern to narrate theologically and faithfully what we were encountering with Christians in the parish. This language avoids a sense of external imposition in an arena where the Holy Spirit is already at work, while also taking seriously the vocation of the church as sign and servant of God's design for the world.[8]

As an expression of apostolicity, excavation and reweaving belong together. Discerning and paying close attention to that which is already of Christ, taking time to prayerfully uncover its dynamics in pastoral care and

As an expression of apostolicity, excavation and reweaving belong together.

the building of friendship and trust, while also reweaving the threads of life, hope and fear into a broader and richer pattern of transformation, discipleship and praise, which can be fed back into the worshipping life of the Church, offered eucharistically for the life of the world. To borrow from George Pace, this method offers a 'workshop for worship'.

The weaving project

The tight closeness of each thread renders counting the number of individual weaves a tricky task. But there are hundreds of individual strands that make up the Wythenshawe Weave. When the loom was transported to the various locations around the community, we invited people to answer three simple questions as they wove their story into the communal artwork.

Three questions arose in conversation with the wider Estates Theology Group, which we decided to pose to each participant, profoundly rooting the project in the locality itself. These were:

- What do you love about this place?
- What gives you grief here?
- What can the church be for you here?

Analysing people's answers from a straightforward questionnaire, we noticed that responses could often be grouped under Trinitarian themes of creation, redemption and sanctification. Not everyone answered these questions, but nearly 50 people did, and their comments, reflections and responses are presented here with some preliminary interpretation, gathered into themes that are faithful to the tone and dynamic of the conversations.

Creation: What do you love about this place?

To this first question, most people replied with comments about the wider community and place of Wythenshawe. A few people spoke in a more focused way about the churches themselves, and there were a small number of outlying responses that ranged widely from 'everything' to 'nothing', and the perhaps more intriguing response of 'better men'! But by far the strongest response, both in number and in depth of feeling, was about the people of Wythenshawe and their sense of community and relationship. Some simply wrote 'community' or 'people', but many clarified this by explaining the kindness of others, the spirit of residents and the readiness of people to support and watch out for one another, to talk and to listen. The responses did not duck the challenges of Wythenshawe but were framed through the eyes of hope, with a love for the experience of living here. One person wrote of what they love about this place: 'the people: through all the ups and downs, the spirit prevails'.

Although the majority of the responses focused on people and relationships within the community, for many the geography of the place itself was worthy of comment. A number of answers included the word 'green' or 'greenery', with more than a nod to Wythenshawe's origins as a garden city: 'the parks', 'the trees and flowers', 'the open spaces' and 'the garden city landscape'. For some this sense of pride in the place was explicit, and for others the place was beautiful because of a blend of people and landscape; the proximity of good hospitals, schools and neighbourhood facilities which helped a community come together for support as well as friendship and social activities. The givenness of place, neighbours and community shone through.

> It is the people and the friendships, relationships and interactions between them that offer the first response to the question of love.

The question, 'What do you love about Wythenshawe?' might appear to emphasize the physical location, the here and the now. Yet an overwhelming majority of responses centred not on the physical place *per se* but on the people who inhabit, reside and bring that space into community. It is the people and the friendships, relationships and interactions between them that offer the first response to the question of love. These interpersonal associations might be based on a sociable, friendly relationship or they might be drawn from a pressing need for support (to be listened to, to watch over, to look out for), but apart from one response, all were positive about people and place. The collective image revealed by these responses is one of a strong community, rooted in its locality and aware of its environment. A community *created*, proud of itself and its life.

Redemption: What gives you grief here?

It might not come as a surprise that the answers to this second question were not only more diverse but often lengthier. To the first question many responded with one or two words, but with this second set of comments about grief, fears and frustrations, we read lists rather than words, alongside sharper, fuller answers outlining situations in greater detail. Once again, the replies to this question were weighted more toward people than place – relationships, and the tensions, challenges and anger of living in close community featured sharply. Even the responses that highlighted problems with the physical place and the environment were framed not as critical of the place itself, but rather of how people treated one another or lived within that place.

By far the largest concern centred on the perception of crime within the community. For some this was predominantly focused on violent crime and drugs; for others it was burglary or vandalism. Underpinning most of it was an element of fear, sadness or anger at antisocial behaviour. The fear of crime is not only linked to the loss of personal belongings, but it also affects security, well-being and the freedom to live safely in the community. Alongside these fears were a large number of comments referring to crimes against the environment, with half of those completing the questionnaire mentioning litter, fly-tipping or 'dog poo' as a source of grief and frustration.

As if to contradict the positive comments about people and relationships uncovered through the first question, many people spoke about tensions between themselves and neighbours, friends and other residents. These comments were more than simple exhaustion at broadly antisocial behaviour and centred on the drama created by particular people in their day-to-day lives, resulting in 'bitchiness', 'back stabbing', 'rudeness' or siding with others in a discriminatory or erratic way. This discrimination was highlighted by one respondent who directed our attention to the institutional bias experienced from managers at a local place of employment. At the heart of many of these comments was a longing for expressions of human dignity, especially when the prejudice, anger or jealousy of a group – no matter how small – seems to undermine that dignity.

A further focus within these comments was less about the people and place itself but rather focused on external pressures that disrupted any stability or continuity. The 'bad press', 'negative feeling' and lack of facilities (for young, old, families or individuals) were recorded with some resignation and frustration. Even when opportunities and aspirations were acknowledged, they were not taken or appreciated. These frustrations were often linked to the problems of crime and antisocial behaviour we have already described, leading to 'unruly kids', the 'place going down', 'lost young children', and that there were 'not enough police'.

Wythenshawe's residents' answers about what gives them grief broadly fall into two categories: crime and negativity. Crime is against either people or property, with varying degrees of seriousness but always violating the safety and security of individuals and the wider community. It is experienced both as personal frustration and a tear in the corporate fabric otherwise so precious to many residents. The negativity was also divided into two broad categories. First, negativity from relationships and broken friendships alongside the tensions and arguments of living within the community formed a substantial counterpoint of grief for many participants in the weaving project. But this sits alongside the negativity projected on to the neighbourhood from outside (especially by the press,

There is a strong sense of being 'done to', misunderstood and unfairly treated.

police or other authorities), or that which is perceived as a lack of opportunity, investment or care from those who have the power to make a difference. In each of these areas the grief was, in all responses, caused by events or activities felt to be outside the control of the individual. There is a strong sense of being 'done to', misunderstood and unfairly treated.

Sanctification: What can the church be for you here?

The third of our questions elicited the greatest variety of answers, very few of which repeated word for word those of others. However, obvious themes again emerged, this time around four areas. The first was that the church is and ought to be a community of love and friendship.[9] Some people described this community as a family and a place of companionship – relationships being key to the local church's values – and one respondent simply wrote, 'Warm!' followed by the name of one of the parish churches which has suffered for decades from seriously inadequate heating! Even this friendly jibe points toward the importance of the church as a welcoming place, with the physical warmth of the building helping to support the emotional and spiritual warmth of those who gather there. The church's reputation as a place of warmth and community clearly enabled its role in the very real concerns to 'fight isolation, support unemployment [and] create well-being'.

The theme of the church as a place of relationship was developed by many who described it in what we might think of as spiritual or theological terms. Many people indicated that the church is a 'refuge', 'a safe place', 'a rock', 'a place of peace', and somewhere that will always be there 'when we need it'. As such, the church – whether a building or its people – was described as much more than a social centre for social needs, and evidently held a particular place in sanctifying and resourcing the spiritual and emotional needs of the community.[10] One person described the church as

26

'a place to think'. Perhaps the most striking answer, which holds together both the tough reality of daily life alongside a robust sense of hope, came from someone who replied to the question with, 'A miracle: I pray for one every night.'

There was much interest expressed in the everyday provision of the church's practical ministry through the help, support and signposting offered to the community. Mention was made of the church's breakfast clubs and social groups and as a place to find support and information when in need ('help find me a flat'). Allied to this were a couple of responses which indicated that finding the support they needed from the church was as 'a place to breathe when we need somewhere else to get away from home', and as a 'place of hope' where they could 'share any worries without judgement'. One respondent was even more direct in asking the church to 'make people happy'.

Finally, three responses deserve a particular mention for their ambivalence. Only one person replied to the question with the words, 'I don't know.' But two individuals, using a similar tone, spoke of their disconnection from the church: 'Not sure been away from it for so long,' and, 'I've been away for too long.' In the sample of those leaving written replies, nobody suggested that the church had no place in the local community, or that the church should simply do nothing for those around it. Those who did not know what the church could be for them, or who did not connect with church, still hinted at a place for it in the community. We encountered no wholesale rejection. Those who have not left the church but simply feel 'away' from it represent what may be quite a large number of people for whom perhaps a return or reconnection is a possibility.

The vast majority of these answers . . . draw their energy and hope from a vision beyond the demands and repeated patterns of everyday life.

The vast majority of these answers articulate a form of longing, for home, space, warmth and safety. They draw their energy and hope from a vision beyond the demands and repeated patterns of everyday life.

Conclusion

The Garden City described in Revelation 21 is a vision of the New Jerusalem, the transformed space where God will eternally be 'at home' among mortals. Tears will be wiped away; death, mourning and pain will be no more; the gates will be open (no need for protection from raids or crime); and at the centre of it all is the Lamb – the one who has offered his life so that humanity might experience the complete joy of being at home with God. But the presence of both the Lamb and the Tree of Life remind us, too, not only of Eden where it all began, but also of the fall, and of the garden of Calvary. The New Jerusalem may represent the consummation of all things in Christ, but it is not an alternative reality where the past is ignored or papered over. This is the fulfilment of longing, an honest consummation which takes the past and its trauma seriously while celebrating the victory of God in Christ, which is stronger than anything the world can throw at it.

Reflecting on this project, we tried hard not to over-synthesize material. Similarly, we did not ever attempt to direct conversations in an artificial way. Our 'excavation' alongside those we spoke to is relatively raw. The 'reweaving' continues to happen in the ongoing life of the parish – voices heard, relationships built, situations of fear held in honest prayer.

The Wythenshawe Weave contains five solitary scarlet threads. At the end of the weaving project, these threads were identified to be added to the final product, representing the five wounds of the crucified Christ. From start to finish, the entire weaving project was approached democratically and openly, and yet the congregation asked the priests of the parish to weave in these wounds. A critic might argue this reveals a kind of clericalism at the heart of the church's life here – anyone who knows the place knows better. The point is that the clergy are frequently those who are visible, recognizable representatives of what the church stands for and seeks. They are those who bury the dead, comfort the sick, broker healing in angry relationships. Above all, they celebrate the sacraments of baptism and Eucharist, preaching reconciliation in a culture where all too frequently life can seem a zero-sum game. At the heart of all the joys and sorrows, frustrations and hopes of this parish are the life-giving wounds of Christ. Such theological reflection is not intended to somehow 'tidy up' what we heard and discussed – if anything, these life-giving wounds continually disrupt the narrative, posing the challenge of the gospel again and again.

Many of those who participated in the Weave asked what would become of it. That it would be displayed in William Temple Church was a source of pride and pleasure for many who would not regard themselves as regulars. But more than that, it was to be hung behind the altar in the Transfiguration Chapel, where the Eucharist is regularly offered; the warp and weft of hundreds of individual stories finding their own place within the offering of Christ, so that we might together be at home with God. That is perhaps the real icon of reweaving: all that has been excavated re-contextualized and held in relationship deep in the sacrificial love of Christ.

So many of those we spent time with during this project were not practising Christians. Many of them found it moving to know that this weave would find its home in their community's holy place. But for those faithful members of the church, the placing of the tapestry behind the altar was deeply symbolic of the church's particular vocation in society. The faithful congregation of William Temple Church know that their role in that community is not only one of compassionate engagement but also one of intercession. Prayer and action unveiling the Garden City which is still to come, perhaps especially in situations where it seems particularly far off.

Our open invitation to Wythenshawe's residents to contribute a thread to the Weave was an act of solidarity which enabled deep and careful listening. The metaphors that accompanied our work and helped us make theological sense of the project – excavation and reweaving – were not a strategy designed to develop outcomes or measurable results. They were just a way of the church being

This was an exercise in building communion, allowing tapestries of relationship to be enlarged and enriched, the church seeking first to hear rather than speak.

the church, rooted in a community for encounter and transformation in Christ. This was an exercise in building communion, allowing tapestries of relationship to be enlarged and enriched, the church seeking first to hear rather than speak.

In due course, there is a danger that the Wythenshawe Weave will just become a memento of a past project. It's all too easy for any kind of church art to become straightforwardly decorative rather than excitingly iconic. But it would certainly be the hope of those involved with this project that the Weave's presence in the Transfiguration Chapel continues to do two things. First, that it symbolizes the ongoing silent intercession for each and every person and story represented within the piece of art. Let it be something that gathers diverse and unedited stories before God, and deeply symbolizes the daily prayer made for sanctification and reconciliation. Second, those involved with this project of partnership with a diverse local community hope that the theological methodology symbolized by the Weave and its conversations might help to shift the dial on wider conceptions of mission and evangelism. It appeared to us that people recognize the gifts of creation and human sociality, they understand about the frailty of sin all too well, and they intuitively know what the church is for.

This is a vision of embedded, committed parish life which relearns the gospel through engagement with those around and seemingly outside it. It is for the wider church to celebrate this, and to honour those ordinary people who have refreshed our vision and taught us again to look for the New Jerusalem.

3

Twydall: From here to the church

ANN RICHARDSON AND JUSTIN STRATIS

It was truly our pleasure to have taken part in this project over the past few years. Our task, as the title of this volume indicates, was to 'find the treasure' of the gospel as it is present in the small Medway town of Twydall through conversations and encounters with its residents and churchgoers. Through extended periods of listening and exploring, we experienced a profound sense of gratitude for the openness and wisdom of Twydall's people as they painted for us a multi-hued picture of life on the estate and reminded us of the power and peace of God's presence in and among a particular community. Though she has since moved on, Ann was the vicar of Holy Trinity Twydall for the duration of the project, and Justin was Tutor in Christian Doctrine at Trinity College Bristol – though he too has now moved on. Together, we have sought to respond the question put to us by the project leaders: 'What is the good news in Twydall Estate?' and this essay could perhaps be read as one particular answer.

This essay proceeds in four sections. First, we offer a description of the parish estate itself, including, briefly, its history, geography and a bit about the local church. Second, we describe the process of producing the 'Twydall Declaration', a series of affirmations and rejections meant to reflect the convictions of Holy Trinity's congregation and which perhaps represents the most significant fruit of our engagement with this project. Third, we offer a brief theological reflection, based largely on Paul's first letter to the

Corinthians, that captures a particular Christian truth that we believe Twydall highlights especially well. Our suggestion is that the kind of sociality formed by the Holy Spirit invites us to imagine the relationship between the churches in terms of mutual interdependence, rather than rank and hierarchy. Fourth and finally, we conclude with a 'Twydallian ecclesiology', a proposal for how we might consider the doctrine of the church in light of Jesus' claim that 'the last will be first, and the first will be last' (Matt. 20.16).

Introduction to Twydall parish

Twydall is a housing estate on the outskirts of Gillingham in the Medway towns. It is home to around 10,500 people from a variety of backgrounds. The estate was built in the 1940s to 1960s, predominantly to relocate families from the Brompton area of Chatham and Gillingham, who were living in substandard housing and supporting Chatham Dockyard – the most significant employer in the area. The Dockyard closed in 1982, an event that had a great and lasting effect in Twydall – not just on employment opportunities, but also on identity, friendship, leisure and aspiration.

There are large numbers of people who have lived in Twydall for their whole lives, people who moved on to the estate when it was new and then raised their families there in large, well-built houses with big gardens and places for their children to meet and play together. More than 15 per cent of Twydall's housing stock – which mostly consists of semi-detached and terraced housing – is now occupied by single people over the age of 65, frequently the last remaining family member of those early residents. Often, children didn't move far to raise families of their own, so entire generations of Medway families might be within a few streets of one another. This means that, within the estate, the entire history of Twydall is carried from its earliest beginnings up to the present day.

These days, only about one-third of the properties are social housing, with one-third being privately rented and one-third owner occupied, but Twydall is still one of Medway Council's most significant locations for council tenants.

As is frequently the case, the estate is geographically quite clearly boundaried. There are dual carriageways on two sides and a railway line on a third. Only at the Rainham end does the estate blend naturally into surrounding housing. This can make it feel very much as though there is one route in and out. It would be a mistake to try to make assumptions about who lives in these homes.

While according to the deprivation indices, the parish falls in the bottom 15 per cent in England, the wealth gap in Twydall is quite wide. Absolute financial poverty is less acute than some of the less-visible kinds, such as poverty of education or opportunity.

Right in the centre of Twydall is Twydall Green – once actually a green, now a car park – surrounded on three sides by a still quite thriving collection of shops, and on the fourth by Holy Trinity Church.

The church building is iconic and quite unique and, whether you love it or loathe it, there is no mistaking whose church it is. It 'belongs' to Twydall and its history is bound up with that of the community, for which it is the largest and most obvious landmark. Walking through the streets of the parish, not a day would go by when I (Ann) did not meet someone who had been baptized, attended school harvest and Christmas services, been a choirboy or youth group member or got married there. Plans to demolish the church building in 2009, since it is no longer used for services owing to many structural problems, led to enough of a local outcry to see the building spot-listed by Heritage England.

The church means something in its local community, whether or not people attend services Sunday by Sunday, and the regular members of the congregation are very aware of the legacy that is entrusted to them by their friends and neighbours as they carry on their work as disciples, community builders and evangelists in the Twydall of the twenty-first century.

When we began this project in 2017, tasked by the Estates Theology Group to consider what the good news might be in, from and for Twydall, we quite quickly uncovered a great sense of joy, hope and determination from this small but confident church community who value one another, are passionate in prayer and warmly, enthusiastically open to all that God might do through them to bless the community in which they live, work and worship. Through half a dozen visits over 18 months, we met in homes, in church, in school and in Twydall's only local pub to talk to churchgoers and local people about the hopes, fears and challenges of living on the estate in these days. We talked to those who have been in Twydall since before the 'new' church was built in 1964, to those who have more recently moved to the estate and to some of Twydall's children and youth, all of whom have their own perspective on life here and on the good news Twydall has to share with the wider church.

One of the things that became clear was that it is hard to get your voice heard more widely when you are a Christian in a small church on an estate on the outskirts of a post-industrial town. And yet, the people of Twydall have things to say that are worth hearing. So began the journey toward the Twydall Declaration – six statements about the things that matter to the people of Holy Trinity and which they would want the church and those who lead it to know.

The people of Twydall have things to say that are worth hearing.

The Twydall Declaration

One of the dangers we were keen to avoid in our encounter with Twydall was the tendency to view estates in general and deprived areas in particular as 'mission fields' that are reliant on the pity and/ or charity of the 'broader' (i.e., richer) churches in order for the gospel to take root. On the contrary, as we spent time conversing with the residents, it became evident just how much these are people who *love* their community and wanted to highlight to Justin in particular just how special it is. Of course, they are not ignorant of the problems they face; talking to the youth in particular revealed a somewhat less-rosy picture of life in Twydall than the impression given by some of the older residents (mostly around the areas of how safe they felt in the streets and how much they had to look forward to in their futures). Nevertheless, each one was plainly proud of his or her town, with very few adult members expressing a desire to ever leave.

This same theme was present in Holy Trinity Church itself. Aside from the obvious frustration about the closure of the church building (the congregation now meets in an adjacent hall), the members expressed a deep love for their church, for one another and for those who have nurtured and led them. Each time I (Justin) arrived for a meeting, they rolled out the proverbial red carpet, showing intentional hospitality and accepting me as a fellow disciple, rather than a strange interloper. (By contrast, I've attended some churches faithfully for years before people even remembered my name!) This is a congregation that takes its faith seriously, thinks deeply of its impact and place in the larger community, and prays with fervency like it matters.

As a result, the thought of bringing something *to* Twydall seemed more and more inappropriate as the project went on. Instead, we kept returning to the question, 'How can we shine a spotlight on the God-given wisdom of this congregation and share its spiritual gifts beyond the boundaries of the estate?' In other words, how can those in Twydall bless and support their brothers and sisters in other parishes? The answer we arrived at was the Twydall Declaration.

> 'How can we shine a spotlight on the God-given wisdom of this congregation and share its spiritual gifts beyond the boundaries of the estate?'

It is no secret that the Christian churches in Britain are declining both in number and in influence. In the Church of England, these numbers can often spark a sense of existential dread that few can deny and yet some are still unwilling to face. What is needed, we believe, is not more silver bullet strategies and gimmicks, but for the church to reclaim its prophetic voice, to be directed by its gospel vocation rather than worries about numbers or lack of funds. We felt that this this sort of prophetic vision was just the sort of thing the people of Holy Trinity Church could offer, and so we set about helping them to articulate this through a series of focused conversations and questionnaires.

Inspired by the example of another church's attempt to speak truth in a time of crisis – the Barmen Declaration of 1934 – the Twydall Declaration aims to capture and amplify the deeply held convictions of a single congregation for the benefit of the whole church. To generate the Declaration's content, we asked the congregation to respond to a series of provocative questions:

- What do you think is good about Christianity?
- What do you think is good about the Church of England?
- What troubles you about Christianity as you've experienced it?
- What troubles you about the Church of England?
- What qualities should a really good priest have?
- What qualities should a really good bishop have?
- What do you think senior clergy in the Church of England think about you?
- What should senior clergy know about you?
- What is the most pressing need in the church today as you have experienced it?
- What gives you hope for the future of the church?

Based on the congregation's responses, some individually written and some gleaned in small group settings, Justin drew up a series of affirmations and rejections that reflected certain of the more consistent refrains. The original draft of the declaration was then submitted to the congregation for several rounds of revision, during which certain phrases were changed, augmented or removed, as well as the title being changed from 'Manifesto' to 'Declaration'. In the midst of this revision stage, the congregation were given full veto power over anything that they felt did not reflect their actual views, with the final draft ultimately receiving their approval for publication (in fact, after Ann's departure as vicar in late 2019, the congregation ended up including the Twydall Declaration in their parish profile). The result, we believe, is a powerful word that deserves a wide hearing in the Church of England and beyond.

The Declaration is included as an appendix to this volume, and thus it should be read for itself without too much accompanying commentary from us. Indeed, it is intended as a message from Holy Trinity Church in its own right and should therefore be experienced as such. However, here we draw particular attention to its third article, which we believe strikes an especially prophetic note for the Estates Theology project as a whole:

We affirm that God is with his people who live on housing estates and is already working powerfully amongst us. The kingdom of God has already come near in our midst, and this should be cause for celebration and gratitude amongst the whole people of God.

We reject the notion that social deprivation indicates God-forsakenness and its flip side that financial stability indicates God's blessing. Housing estates are not mere objects for the charity of the rich; they are diverse communities of people across the socio-economic spectrum in which the body of Christ has taken root and in which the Holy Spirit is active.

In a sense, this is the message we felt was being addressed to us most acutely and so served as confirmation of our desire to shepherd the Declaration to publication. In short, it speaks of the fact that estate churches in general and Holy Trinity in particular *are already* sites of divine action and therefore ought to be treated as the holy, sanctified things that they are. To the extent that the wider church neglects to listen to these communities, such is the extent that it experiences an impoverished and truncated vision of God's work in the world. Indeed, God has more for his people than we might expect, and to hear his voice in our midst we must strain our ears in all directions to grasp precisely what the Spirit is saying to the churches, even and perhaps especially when the medium is a small, seemingly insignificant group of saints in a place like Twydall.

Theological reflection: Churches and the economy of the Spirit in 1 Corinthians

No two estates are exactly alike, and so the practical lessons learned from our encounter with Twydall may not necessarily be applied across the board. Therefore, what may be more beneficial is to reflect on some of the *theological* realities that this experience has brought to light, particularly as we've spent time considering the ways in which Tywdall has challenged or expanded our understanding of the Christian church.

The church is not a voluntary social organization. It is not made up of like-minded people drawn together by mutual interest in some common goal or theme. The church, the Scriptures teach us, is the body of Christ, the holy fellowship of the chosen, and so it exists only by divine initiative. As John Webster comments, 'Primarily, to speak of the church as holy is to indicate that it is the assembly of the *elect*.'[1] For this reason, the apostle can say of the church, as was once said of the wandering Israelites, 'You are a *chosen* race, a royal priesthood, a holy nation, God's own people, in order that you may proclaim the mighty acts of him who called you out of darkness into his marvellous light' (1 Pet. 2.9, emphasis mine).

If this is the case, then the usual means of social analysis that we might apply to other sorts of communities can never tell the full story of what the church precisely is. The church is not merely the product of social evolution; the church was *called* into existence, created by the very same Word that once commanded all things to arise from nothing. Likewise, the persistence of the church to its appointed end will not be its own achievement; the church is held in the care of God, safe from the assaults of the evil one, solely because of God's promised presence in its midst. Its steadfastness therefore expresses itself not in fearful busyness driven by the desire for self-preservation, but in hope and trust: 'it draws strength from the power of the risen Lord, to overcome with patience and charity its afflictions and difficulties, from within and from without.'[2]

And so, the church is a society like no other, even as it is made up of people whose lives straddle all the intersecting factors of human existence. This dual reality that sees God's people set in relationship with both the holy and the profane has caused the church occasionally to become dazzled by alternative social models – that is, to conform to certain patterns of relationship that contradict its Christological identity. This is perhaps no more evident than in the case of the first-century church in Corinth.

In 1 Corinthians 11, the apostle Paul records his astonishment at reports that the Christians in Corinth were using the Lord's supper as an occasion for division, rather than unity:

> For when the time comes to eat, each of you goes ahead with your own supper, and one goes hungry and another becomes drunk. What! Do you not have homes to eat and drink in? Or do you show contempt for the church of God and humiliate those who have nothing?
> (1 Corinthians 11.21–22)

While the precise context is debatable, it seems probable that the Roman practice of a tiered system of entertaining was being recreated among the Corinthians, with the top tier gaining access to the eucharistic meal first, and the lesser castes being expected to dine on their own or even later on.[3] Although this practice likely felt normal and natural to the Corinthians (perhaps even to those in the lower classes), Paul rejects it as a profound failure in terms of 'discerning the body' (1 Cor. 11.29), that is, to make visible the Christological reality that 'we who are many are *one* body, for we all partake of the *one* bread' (1 Cor. 10.17, emphasis mine). For Paul, the church is not the church until *all* are regarded as essential for the integrity of the meal. He therefore commands the Corinthians to 'wait for one another' at the holy supper (1 Cor. 11.33, emphasis mine). This was plainly a counterintuitive demand vis-à-vis the predominant socialities of the day, but Paul insists on it precisely because, for him, the Corinthian church was not just a gathering of Greco-Romans around a common religious interest, but a prophetically interruptive new social reality formed around the very presence of Jesus.

This reasoning also forms the basis of Paul's celebrated 'body' metaphor found in 1 Corinthians 12. While in chapter 11, the challenge had to do with the church's conformity to prevailing hierarchical social practices, in chapter 12 we see the ways in which the Corinthians had allowed the assumptions of these practices to seep into their own ecclesial self-understanding. The particular error that Paul identifies concerns the fact that certain spiritual gifts were deemed more valuable than others – a circumstance that led to the marginalization of those whose gifts were considered less 'impactful' for the flourishing of the community. Here, too, Paul criticizes the Corinthians for taking what God intended to be a visible manifestation of unity – the democratization of the Spirit – as yet another occasion for ranking, division and hierarchy. Indeed, he explains, just as all partake of one and the same bread, so *all* of the gifts 'are activated by one and the same Spirit' (1 Cor. 12.11). What should have driven the church toward interdependence through a shared recognition of the one Spirit's ministry became distorted as the Corinthians assumed the right to judge the relative merit of individuals' spiritual contributions.

In response, Paul sets out to correct this flawed calculus. It is not for us to assess the 'value' of particular gifts for the unfolding of God's work in the world. Instead, he says, we are to regard one another as equally crucial, equally essential parts of Christ's body:

As it is, there are many members, yet one body. The eye cannot to say to the hand, 'I have no need of you', nor again the head to the feet, 'I have no need of you.' On the contrary, the

members of the body that *seem* to be weaker are *indispensable*
. . . If one member suffers, all suffer together with it; if one
member is honoured, all rejoice together with it.
(1 Corinthians 12.20–22, 26, emphasis mine)

For Paul, there is no difference between an apostle, a tongues-
speaker, a prophet, a teacher or a healer in terms of the *necessity*
of the contribution each makes to the church. This is because the
exercising of these distinct gifts is primarily the work of the one
Holy Spirit, and thus to elevate certain gifts over others is to divide
and rank the Spirit's ministry as if the Spirit itself could be divided
and ranked – clearly an impossibility.[4]

What Paul is demonstrating, therefore, is an entirely new means
of social analysis, one in which all our 'managerial' calculations of
role and rank become thoroughly
relativized by the unity of the body
actualized by the Spirit. Indeed, the
church – the *one* church – is built
up by the ministry of the *one* Spirit.
Consequently, that which, by
worldly reckoning, may once have been an occasion for hierarchy
(diversity of social contribution) becomes an opportunity for
mutual reliance. Just as Christ joins together Jew and Gentile in
such a way that *difference* becomes the ground of *relationship*
rather than division, so the Spirit distributes various gifts such that
diversity becomes the ground of *unity*.

What Paul is demonstrating . . . is an entirely new means of social analysis.

We suggest that Paul's teaching on the unity in diversity of
spiritual gifts and the social implications of oneness in Christ can
be applied to interchurch relationships as well. It can certainly
feel natural to observe a group of churches and make judgements
about the relative merit of each's ecclesial contribution. In fact,
we might say, this is precisely what a prudent manager ought to
do. Like a CEO surveying the performance data of their various
store branches, a bishop may be inclined to render informal
judgements on the role and rank of particular parishes in the
ministry eco-system of their diocese. Churches deemed to be

particularly 'influential' may be given a more prominent voice in diocesan discussion over strategy, while smaller churches may receive less attention. Likewise, senior clerics might be inclined to take counsel from the more 'successful' clergy, with a more paternalistic attitude directed toward the rank-and-file ministers. While such an approach might be perfectly at home in a modern, managerial context, in the church it reveals a fundamental failure to imagine the new kind of social reality that Paul commends to the Corinthians.

In truth, it is not our responsibility to discern the particular ways in which churches are being used by God to nourish and strengthen the body of Christ. What may seem to us to be a fantastically fruitful ministry may in the end be burned up as so much 'wood, hay, straw', and those we regarded as less significant may be revealed to be overlayed with 'gold, silver, precious stones' that were present all along (1 Cor. 3.11–15).

But we need not paint the situation with such extreme colours. More positively, we ought simply to admit that we cannot know the precise manner in which we rely on one another as individual Christians and as diverse congregations. Dietrich Bonhoeffer's comments on the mutual reliance of Christians in prayer could equally be applied to inter-church relationships:

> As Christians, we cannot boast about our solitary relationship with God. Our strength comes to us from the church-community, and we will never know how much our own prayer accomplished, and what we gained through the fervent intercession of people unknown to us.[5]

Could it be, for instance, that what we might consider to be a diocese's 'flagship' church owes its 'successful' ministry in part to the Spirit's work among people of far lesser-known Christian communities? Would we dismiss the ministry of so many 'insignificant' smaller churches if we could see the profoundly necessary *spiritual* role that these churches play in supporting and upholding the body of Christ at large? Or, as the Corinthians seemed to assume, must all churches be measured against the bar of a single spiritual office (1 Cor. 12.27–30)?

Of course, there are caveats to this perspective. Deference to the mutual interdependence of churches cannot be used as an excuse to avoid *all* kinds of judgements – Paul's very terse commentary on the state of the Corinthian church is surely testament to that. What should be avoided, however, are judgements that pretend to see beyond the veil of the mystery of the Spirit's work, which aim to discern the miraculous from the mundane purely on the basis of perceived 'results' or 'effectiveness'. On the contrary, we must learn, as Paul says, to *wait* for one another, to give all a seat at the table and, above all, to wait for the final revelation of precisely what God was up to in knitting people such as us together in just this way.

Would we dismiss the ministry of so many 'insignificant' smaller churches if we could see the profoundly necessary *spiritual* role that these churches play in supporting and upholding the body of Christ at large?

A Twydallian ecclesiology

Our encounter with the Christians in Twydall was a profoundly encouraging one, if only for what they gave to us. There are people in this parish for whom reading and writing presents an enormous challenge, who are under-educated and who are thoroughly working class, but who pray with a power and depth of prophetic insight that, perhaps in another time, Christians from around the world might have been compelled to travel great distances to sit at their feet and learn of their spiritual practices. Likewise, there are people in Twydall who are well educated, financially comfortable and incredibly well spoken, yet who regard their working-class neighbours as full partners in the gospel without a second thought given to what might in other contexts divide them. There are young people who cling tenaciously to the Lord Jesus Christ despite whatever socio-economic challenges they might currently face and likely will continue to face throughout their lives. And there are newcomers who arrived late to the parish, yet who are welcomed into the community and given space to make their own contribution, as from the Lord. In a word, what we saw in Twydall Parish was a genuine *Christian community* – a church – and such is, of course, the work of the Holy Spirit.[6]

What if, in the Church of England, we retrained ourselves to survey our many parishes, not with a despairing eye to numerical decline, but instead with a sense of expectation that God's promise to never abandon his church is in the midst of being made real in surprising places? What if, instead of pinning our hopes on a select few 'successful' churches, we began the work of discovering resources that we never knew we had but perhaps have been there all along? Of course, doing so may change the look (and sound) of those in the spotlight, but that is precisely the kind of perpetual church re-formation the Holy Spirit drives us to embrace. As Willie Jennings argues, one of the earliest lessons that the church had to learn was that inclusion in the body of Christ means learning how to *see* each other not simply as people competing for finite space, but as objects of desire that lead us to transgress given boundaries. Where once we thought of ourselves as hierarchically related (as the Corinthians did), now we are being taught to love one another in mutual submission, to become something *new*, together. The Christian God, Jennings argues, is 'an erotic God who seeks to place in each of us a desire for those outside of us, outside our worlds of culture, clan, nation, tribe, faith, politics, class, and species'.[7]

What then, is a Twydallian ecclesiology? Simply put, it is an account of the church where Christian communities of all shapes, sizes, classes, geographical locations and unique histories are concretely relied upon to share their spiritual gifts 'for the common good'.[8] As believers in Christ, we need each other – we need each other perhaps more deeply than any other human relationship.

And this means, of course, that the Church of England *needs* Holy Trinity Twydall, in ways that a worldly perspective may not make entirely evident. Indeed, in God's economy, *all* churches are 'resource churches', for all have been given a share in the one Spirit, on whom we rely absolutely for our life and sustenance.

4

Rubery: Borders and boundaries

CLAIRE TURNER

When we are in transitional space, we are neither ourselves as we have come to know nor are we our others. We are in transition. We are traversing the boundaries between self and other and reconfiguring those boundaries and the meanings we give them. We are entertaining strangeness and playing in difference. We are crossing that important internal boundary that is the line between the person we have been but no longer are and the person we will become.[1]

Rubery is a place full of borders and boundaries. A busy dual carriage way cuts the town (known confusingly as a village) in half from East to West, and the invisible yet known boundary between Bromsgrove and Birmingham cuts through the place from north to south. Some families have always lived north of the A38 since its construction in the 1960s; others stick resolutely to the south where, for reasons unknown, property tends to be more expensive. While invisible, the boundary between Birmingham and Bromsgrove is no less imposing. Historically, many chose to move out of the City of Birmingham to Rubery, Bromsgrove, only to find a decade or so later that Birmingham was developing new estates to house those displaced by inner-city slum clearances on their doorsteps. Those who had chosen to move 'out' pushed against the arrival of those who had no such choice. Many still do.

Borders and boundaries weigh heavily in Rubery. Some young people go to the high school on the Birmingham side, others to the high school on the Bromsgrove side. Funding, application processes and health authorities relate to one set of neighbours and not to another. Some local doctors' surgeries refer people to Birmingham hospitals and others to Worcestershire hospitals – the 'postcode lottery' becoming very real for a number of families. The organization that has arranged day trips and Christmas parties for older residents continues to discuss whether those who live on the Birmingham side should be allowed on the coach to Weston-super-Mare. The front desk at the local West Mercia police station, located on the Bromsgrove side of the border, is closed. No doubt many different things would have influenced this decision, but it doesn't seem inappropriate to suggest that the numbers who tried to report alleged crimes taking place on the Birmingham side, thereby needing West Midlands Police, played some small part.

Amid the nonsense and the bureaucracy, borders become rifts, caverns open up and people slip through the gaps.

This is perhaps most notable on the Cock Hill estate which runs along the Birmingham–Bromsgrove border down to the A38. Comprising a large proportion of social housing, this community, squashed as it is onto this invisible corner between two axes, experiences higher rates of child poverty than any other neighbourhood in Birmingham, putting it thirteenth on such a scale nationally.[2] People who live 'over the border' in Bromsgrove report never having walked through the estate; some deny that it is part of Rubery; yet its residents use the same services, have the same postcode, the same sense that they 'live in Rubery' as anyone else.

As a parish church, St Chad's Rubery has tentatively started to ask what it might mean to explore these boundaries – to meet people in the gaps, to play on the borders, to embrace border crossing, to engage in place making in and on the boundaries, to dance on the edges and to invite others to do the same. Might this exploration,

> As a parish church, St Chad's Rubery has tentatively started to ask what it might mean to explore these boundaries . . . to dance on the edges and to invite others to do the same.

or that which emerges from it, enable us to reframe a rift or crack as a transitional space; a space in which, to make reference to Ellsworth once more, we generate possibility and potential as opposed to restricted, bounded responses?[3] Could we even start to make visible or play with what David Tracy might describe as a 'limit experience' – an encounter that reveals something of one's internal narrative in order to disrupt it; an encounter that steps across the boundary between common experience and religious experience, between that which is known and unknown, where 'meaning' becomes 'meaningfulness'?[4]

What happens when we dwell on the border?

In 2017, following a funding application initiated by our then Mission Apprentice, Jodie Brown, St Chad's was awarded £4,500 from Community First Worcestershire's Youth Social Action Fund (Bromsgrove Festival subsequently added £500) to commission an artist to engage a group of young people in an exploration of the borders and boundaries, both real and imagined, in their community. The result of this work was to be some kind of unspecified creative intervention under the A38 flyover, the underpass that marks not only the boundary between north and south but also that between Bromsgrove and Birmingham, east and west. It is, in this way, a pivot point – a rather arresting space but one that marks transition.

The Rubery Youth Club, run by the YMCA, meets at St Chad's Rubery and its members became the project participants. The artist's brief was prepared by the team at St Chad's and distributed to artists via various local networks. However, the young people themselves interviewed and selected the artist – preparing questions and asking them on the day, and offering their opinions and reflections, so that together they could appoint the artist, which actually turned out to be two: Jacqui and David Grange from Creative Solutions.

During spring 2018, the artists spent time with the young people, mapping their community and getting to know them, responding to their energy, inviting them to share how they felt about the place in which they live. Jacqui and David brought with them a creative practice that is rooted in participation. Their source material and their creative tools include conversations and comments, found words and shared experiences alongside paint, cameras and printing presses. Their approach resonates with Nicolas Bourriaud's description in *Relational Aesthetics*: art as an activity that consists of a set of relationships with the world with the help of signs, forms, actions and objects[5] – art as a verb, not a noun. The art existed as much in the process as in the product, in the verbal exchange as much as in the final event.

The mid-point of what became known as The Underpass Project took place in June 2018 during a local community arts weekend. Led entirely by the young people, Jacqui and David conceived with them the 'Flash Floss Feast', a community gathering with food in the underpass, during which visitors would be taught to 'floss' (a dance move). The day saw workshops on the street during which T-shirts were printed and decorations made. In the evening, people wearing floss T-shirts started to gather round tables laden with samosas and sausage rolls under the flyover. Large black silhouettes depicting one of the young people in full floss mode hung on the imposing concrete structure, as would a medieval wall hanging in a religious setting. Music bounced off the industrial surroundings, people met neighbours they hadn't met before, people started to comment that this space could be so much more, could be better used. There was chatting, laughing and dancing. No one was really 'in charge' and not much 'happened', but art was experienced and a place, cathedral-like in its scale and architecture, was made.

The event was followed by more workshops which culminated, on a chilly evening in November 2018, at the 'Funky Flyover Fandango'. Here, emboldened by the first event, church members, YMCA staff, young people and the artists returned to claim and transform the space once more. A pile of screens showed images of the young people, a soundscape broadcast their experiences around the space, UV paint marked out silhouettes on the walls and a vast quantity of hot dogs was served. On arrival, visitors were issued with UV chalk and torches to both write messages and seek them out – stories hidden, stories uncovered. Those added on the night were big and boisterous, proud and loud – but those collected by the young people and transcribed in the invisible chalk by the artists before the event began were altogether quieter, more painful, a little more broken.

At both events, what was once 'non-space' became 'a space'; what was once a dead area came alive. Owned by the young people, held by the artists' practice and initiated by the church, this event began to tentatively interrupt the community's perception of this space and, subsequently, of themselves. Furthermore, that 'interrupting' led us as a church to ask, 'If this space isn't what we thought it was and this boundary not as impermeable as we had assumed, who are we in relation to it?' Did this tentatively start to suggest an emerging model for gathering, assembling, conversing and perhaps even worshipping in and on the edges; prayer on the borders and boundaries that gives context to experience? Perhaps, just perhaps, by listening, playing and being on the edges, we might, together, traverse the boundaries between self and other, reconfiguring those boundaries and, in turn, the meanings we give them.

There exists a plethora of writing on liturgy, worship and the nature of the Christian gathering on which we might draw as we continue to wrestle with these questions. Many, such as liturgist Gordon Lathrop, stress the need to deepen and expand our understanding of God through our worship, and while he may never have envisioned the space under a dual carriageway, Lathrop's work expresses a yearning for this to happen wherever and whenever we gather. His trilogy, *Holy Things*, *Holy People* and *Holy Ground*, espouses a theology based on broken symbol, juxtaposition and ordo, the shape and rhythm of the liturgy.[6] For him, just as it is for liturgists as diverse as Benjamin Gordon-Taylor[7]and Robert Hovda,[8] the primary symbol of the liturgical gathering is the gathering, the assembly, itself.[9] During the gathering, the assembly encounters broken symbols, an idea Lathrop draws from Paul Tillich's idea of the 'broken myth',[10] a myth that is both true and, owing to the inadequacy of the language used to tell it, also wrong, thereby only capable of speaking truth by referencing something beyond itself.[11]

David Tracy, who also draws on Tillich's work, albeit in different ways, would agree, suggesting as he does that it is as problematic to take myths literally as it is to see religious metaphors as substitutes for literal meaning.[12] Myths, as do the visual arts, do something more by operating on the edges of meaning, by revealing the 'not quite' nature of our understanding. Cutting through these somewhat abstract ideas is Michael Perham, who describes the symbolic nature of this gathering as simply arriving as people, becoming congregation and, together, discovering a new corporate identity.[13]

While neither the Flash Floss Feast nor the Funky Flyover Fandango sought or claimed to be acts of worship, they both involved the intentional gathering of an assembly to discover together something of what was and what might be. They both involved engagement with a number of visual symbols or clues that pointed to something that was 'beyond'; both required participation and collaboration and, during both, the space for such engagement was 'held' by a facilitator or president, in this case the artist. In addition, while a framework for collaboration had been drawn by the artists, neither event predetermined what type of transient community might form that evening or, indeed, the nature of the space that would be created as a result. This does not mean these events weren't carefully and thoughtfully planned or that they weren't rooted in the artists' own established practice. Rather, the framework for engagement and the symbols used enabled collaboration and discovery.

Cláudio Carvalhaes' recent book, *What's Worship Got to Do with It? Interpreting Life Liturgically*,[14] is critical of traditional liturgical patterns and models. Carvalhaes seeks to find new ways of creating liturgy together and to break down the hierarchical power structures that can all too often be observed in our churches. Introducing the text, Paul Galbreath hopes it will encourage us to create and offer liturgy that takes account of different local sources, diverse languages, perspectives and life experiences;[15] liturgy that cherishes the 'existential and confessional' forms of our neighbours' lives[16] by juxtaposing that which we have traditionally called holy with those special and particular things that are never named as such.[17] Interestingly, Galbreath and Carvalhaes both assert that Lathrop's quest to reveal and indeed share the deep liturgical patterns of inherited Christian worship somehow negate their task. However, Lathrop has stated that when we root ourselves in the ordo, the deep liturgical structures of our worship, we are more able (not less) to open the door, to acknowledge and embrace the diversity of cultural gifts, the diverse patterns of assembling and departing of our worshippers and to set our gathering in the midst of God's world.[18] He affirms Robert Hovda's desire to 'give away' our symbols so that they become bigger and more accessible,[19] and references writers such as John Steinbeck who used symbols to clear or mark out the ground in order that something new could be discovered.[20] Reading Carvalhaes' descriptions of the gatherings that he has enabled and participated in, on the margins and at the edges of our communities, he does just that.

What, then, of the symbols found at or exposed by our very particular border? And having identified our borders as creative, fertile places, how do we nurture the sense that they may be places of meeting and transition as opposed to barriers and obstacles? How do we reclaim the border from the sense that it is a disorienting, liminal space of endings and hard-won beginnings[21] and instead embrace the creativity inherent in transition?

Listening to people share their stories of living on the Cock Hill estate is a gift – often challenging, always humbling, but certainly a gift. The stories often describe ill health, family circumstances, employment or financial pressures and the impact such experiences have had and continue to have on individuals. There are stories of addiction, violence, poverty and family trauma – but also of friendship and community, of neighbours stepping in when the support system fails, of trust and of the 'shining lights' who lift up those who fall down. This is not a place that needs someone to arrive from across the border and 'fix' something; the church community **This is not a place that needs someone to arrive from across the border and 'fix' something.** cannot assume that it has something not already present and active on the border, on the estate. These places on the margins, these 'edge places', offer as much as they 'need', and what is 'needed' is often the practical resources, not the ideas or the enthusiasm or the desire for transformation.

Likewise, while the church clearly has a story to tell, it is not a different story from the one found on the estate; the Christian story is in itself an 'invitation into liminality'.[22] Christians hope for the kingdom, made present in Jesus Christ but not yet complete – we are always in between, in liminal space, and yet we don't label this state of being as negative. Rather, we speak of this in-between time as one of discovery; of actively seeking, growing and yearning. We use positive words to describe the Christian experience of liminality but are so often in danger of naming the transitional, liminal, transient nature of our estates as negative. In turn, by labelling something as undesirable, we rush to 'fix' as opposed to listen; to speak as opposed to receive. By negatively naming something as 'unstable' or impermanent we are in danger of creating an unhealthy self-fulfilling prophecy. We return again to my question above: 'How do we reclaim the border from the sense that it is a disorienting, liminal space of endings and hard-won beginnings[23] and instead embrace the creativity inherent in transition?'

The first step toward an answer might be to recognize the different 'assemblies' already present on our borders. The two collaborative arts events described above did not happen in a vacuum but were born out of relationships that had developed over time. The specific nature of the gathering was both unique and new but the inherent, deep-rooted sense of community, the wider assembly, was already present. In hosting the event and 'holding' the space for it to take place, the church's subconscious, unnamed understanding of the importance of the assembly, of *ekklesia*, shone a light on what was already there: life, community, creativity, desire.

Over the centuries, the words *ekklesia* (assembly) and 'church' have become rather synonymous, but to gather, to assemble, suggests something that anyone can do, in any place and at any time. The place does not need to be 'special' (the flyover was definitely not special), but the specialness of the ordinary things, of the local people, of the food that is served, is worth celebrating. Returning to Lathrop, we hear his cry for the rediscovery of 'assembly', not just as the primary symbol for our worshipping life but as the means through which we invite the Holy Spirit to shape and form us.[24] From this point, it is not too far a leap to arrive at a place where some kind of liturgy on or for the margins might emerge – not too fanciful to see the forgotten spaces in and on our estates as spaces in which 'interwoven, mutually reinterpreting, mostly biblical, always engaging, almost always metaphoric, verbal and enacted and then sometimes visual images'[25] create the opportunity to:

read and interpret those sacred stories of our community,
so that they speak a word to people today;
to remember and practise those rituals and rights of
    meaning
that in their poetry address humanity at the level where
change operates;
to foster in community through word and sacrament
that encounter with truth which will set people free
to minister as the body of Christ.[26]

5

Eltham: The limits of being Christian

NICK RUSSELL AND CARLTON TURNER

Introduction: Beyond a binary view

The classic view of Christian community is of people who know Jesus and have taken a conscious decision to be his disciples. In the Acts of the Apostles, we see Peter preaching and requiring that his hearers, 'Repent, and be baptized . . . in the name of Jesus Christ so that your sins may be forgiven; and you will receive the gift of the Holy Spirit' (Acts 2.38). In the New Testament letters, there are many echoes of this. Furthermore, a distinction is made between insiders and outsiders: 'Do not be mismatched with unbelievers. For what partnership is there between righteousness and lawlessness? Or what fellowship is there between light and darkness?' (2 Cor. 6.14). In this view, those who belong to the church have all the light and those outside are in darkness. There is nothing to be gained or learned from those outside the church.

It is this strict binary conception of the church itself that hinders its ministry. The reality in mission, however, is that those outside the church, especially among the poorest, have a lot to teach. Edward Pusey said, 'the poor are the wealth . . . of the Church'.[1] Gustavo Gutiérrez makes the point that the church is enriched theologically by the lens through which the poor interpret the Bible.[2] But what the poorest in Britain have to contribute goes much further than this into the moral realm.

This chapter reflects on the experience of ministry in South East London in Church Army's Greenwich Centre of Mission (Eltham and Kidbrooke). The major theme arising from this particular urban estate ministry is that there often exists an exemplary standard of generosity and mutual care and practical support in the unchurched community. In fact, it is this way of life amid the ongoing traumas of urban priority contexts that tends to recapture often-forgotten aspects of Jesus' ministry and early conceptions of what it means to be the church in the world. Jesus and his earliest disciples inhabited a movement that defied binary constructs of all types, particularly looking to social, political, cultural and even ecclesiastical margins as sites of renewal and transformation.

With this in mind, we will continue with the following: first, we will take a deeper dive into stories from Eltham and Kidbrooke. Second, we will explore what we consider to be a 'toxic evangelism' that perpetuates the binary approach to church and community engagements, particularly in estate contexts. Finally, we will explore what we refer to as 'the limits of being Christian'. Ministry on estates challenges the criteria by which we can call a person a Christian or not. In other words, are those who demonstrate the love of God any less Christian than those who make a formal declaration or participate in ecclesiastical spaces? Stated another way, is Jesus only revealed by those within the church? Can he not also be revealed by those outside its walls?

Eltham and Kidbrooke: A case study

Eltham and Kidbrooke are ex-factory, White working-class estates that have struggled to integrate other cultures and ethnicities. Currently, it is more tolerant than it used to be, but there is still an underlying sentiment of this. There is a historic presence of the English Defence League (EDL) in the area and, in fact, it was in this geographical space that Stephen Lawrence was killed in 1993. Naturally, in this context, joblessness, poverty and deprivation, relationship toxicity, family strain and low educational attainment are realities. The communities also struggle with drug use, drug turf wars and the increasing exposure of young people to drug use or drug-pushing. An associated estate, the Ferrier Estate, was actually demolished because of its high incidences of crime, violence, social breakdowns, etc, but only to make way for the building of a new estate that has in effect resulted in 'social cleansing'.

Some of the estates in the Eltham area are open and more accessible. Eltham is where people would come to do their shopping. Others in the parish, like Horn Park, are not: accessible by one bus and with one way into and one way out of the estate. It is enclosed, and it was in this space that a mental institution was built.

Nick Russell, a Church Army officer (and co-author of this chapter), has carried out a ministry to directly respond to the issues within Eltham and Kidbrooke. His work, along with his team, addresses vulnerable adults, children excluded from school, youth ministry for children on the estates, and the use of volunteers who are ex-offenders or young people trying to get back into work. His church, St Saviour's, is more than 50 per cent African. This contrasts with the 76 per cent or so White British make-up of the Middle Park and Sutcliffe Ward,[3] with Middle Park and Horn Park having the preponderance of the White population. The church building itself looks like a fortress designed to keep people out, even though it has a certain interior beauty which is impossible to imagine from the outside, so that it tends to exclude the uninitiated and non-members. It was built in about 1930, architecturally self-indulgent and deliberately forbidding, without any thought for the preferences of the workers whose homes surrounded it. It is tall and impossibly expensive to heat in winter, an imposition on, rather than a gift to, local working-class people. It conveys the impression of an over-confident patrician church institution that believed it knew best and cared little about the needs and feelings of the poor – in contrast to the attitude expressed so often by Jesus.

Nick and his team minister among unchurched people in deprived communities in Eltham and Kidbrooke, recruiting volunteers and workers from these. These volunteers and workers have very little knowledge of Christianity, not even a basic knowledge or understanding of Easter, for example. In the binary view of many in the church, they are 'not saved'. However, the image of a loving and caring God is often strongly present, and the levels of generosity and commitment to projects of practical care and love often exceed those of church members. The witness of these unchurched workers is one in which they are united in the transforming of their local community through a kind of selfless love best described in 1 Corinthians 13. The community, though bearing many scars, works hard to grow in wholeness.

Nick explains that in one of their projects, Superkidz, where they run training sessions for carers and for young people, they find that the beneficiaries, young people and adults, inevitably refocus and reframe the way ministry is done.

In speaking of scars and trauma, the level of suffering and the psychological damage done to people in our poorest communities is underestimated. During a training session in Eltham about domestic violence, seven out of eight women sitting around the table had experienced domestic violence, often over a long period. Some had reported the problem to the police, only for the partner to be cautioned and then to return to wreak vengeance. The daily stress of difficult experiences like this, or of not having enough money to feed children, or of having no heating during winter, or of facing endless series of difficulties, can result in depression, and a condition described by Martin Seligman as 'learned helplessness'.[4] In experiments that would not nowadays be allowed, Seligman in the 1960s showed that dogs in an electric shock experiment did not try to escape even though this was possible if they had initially been given no option but to suffer. Even though in a subsequent experiment they had an option to escape, they did not try. There was a deep-seated conclusion that nothing could be done. This is similar to estate contexts where many have no confidence in their ability to make things better, and slide into despair and depression. Zero-hours contracts that end suddenly and pay late, coupled with the failures of Universal Credit, can mean unexpected reductions in income that take weeks to put right. Saving for this kind of eventuality is impossible.

One of the worst aspects of psychological damage in deprived communities is seen in what Bowlby called the 'Internal Working

Model', a set of unconsciously held assumptions about ourselves and other people.[5] It is like a distorting lens, making others seem hostile and powerful and, like a distorting mirror, making the self seem worthless and powerless. In teenage boys it often leads to unreasonably aggressive behaviour. In girls it tends to lead to vulnerability to seeking any kind of affirmation, including the false affirmation that comes from a boy wanting sex. It is a psychological truism that unconditional and unwavering, persevering love restores this lens and mirror and removes the distortions. This precludes a binary approach where people are excluded from the community because of bad behaviour. This does not mean that bad behaviour isn't challenged, but the fundamental approach is a loving affirmation of the person, keeping them included in the group.

A more concrete example of ministry in Eltham and Kidbrooke is the difficulty being faced with youth violence and knife crime. Where children have grown up in fear or severe insecurity, there is often an under-developed ability to empathize, so a victim is somehow seen as 'other', with little ability on the part of the attacker to put themselves in the victim's position, or the bereaved family's position. For such young people, empathy can be restored through caring, secure relationships and cognitive mentoring. There are biological factors at play too: conscious self-control mechanisms in the brain are often weakened by cortisol if there are persistent high levels of stress in childhood, caused, for example, by fear or insecurity in carer–child relationships, domestic violence and so on. If love and belonging are maintained over a sufficient period by the mission community, the effect of long-term infant and childhood stress is reduced.

Nick and his team also teach the tackling of three kinds of ignorance: ignorance of the physical effects of stabbing someone; ignorance of the uncontrolled way the mind works in a fight, bypassing conscious self-control; ignorance of the legal punishments that result. All of these things can be addressed cognitively, including through presentations and posters, but this is only effective once trust has been gained through inclusive love and

The loving missional community is . . . perhaps the most effective way of tackling serious youth violence.

acceptance. The loving missional community is a positive substitute, perhaps the most effective way of tackling serious youth violence. The approach to youth work in Eltham and Kidbrooke is highly relational; both group and individual mentoring are used at club meetings.

In the midst of what can only be described as a traumatic context of ministry, the following are examples of a kind of generosity and compassion that exceeds easy classifications and binary distinctions. First, Nick recalls a young mother addicted to cocaine:

She came to us as a youth in our youth clubs, and we gave her a work experience place as a trainee youth support worker. She was brought up in a household where there was alcohol abuse and violence directed at her mother and herself. Two of her brothers deal drugs and one is in prison. Her first partner has special needs and a congenital disease, and her care for him brought them together. Sadly, he became violent towards her and their relationship broke down. Some of her closest friends are addicts and she became a cannabis and then a cocaine user, with increasing dependency. We have finally managed to engage her in a drug rehabilitation project.

What we have seen in her is an immediate response of care and compassion to anyone in need, regardless of her own difficulties. One of our youths was stabbed and ended up in King's Hospital. She was the first at his bedside. Her new partner is a chronic pain sufferer, and whatever her problems, his needs always come first.

He continues with another example:

Among those we have helped through our youth charity is a mother with extensive experience of domestic violence.

She constantly had to move when her ex-partner discovered the location of the homes provided by the Council. This left her with depression and anxiety, with Social Services on the brink of removing her children from her, partly because of the unhygienic living conditions in her home, which were also deepening her depression, reducing her ability to parent. Without being prompted, a team of our local parents arrived on her doorstep to clean and decorate her home. Social Services were reassured by their support and the mother, who has now made a complete recovery, is a valued youth support worker and a devoted volunteer at one of our fresh expressions of church. She is resourceful, and constantly full of ideas for the work of the mission. She supports others in their needs and her ability to use a computer in an area where nearly 40 per cent of people have no qualifications at all and most welfare is accessed online is extremely valuable.

To see church and unchurched in a morally binary way is entirely false.

Evangelism and toxic binariness

Reflecting on the relationship between the church and the surrounding estates in Eltham and Kidbrooke, we find that the binary between church and estate 'is' the problem. Sharp distinctions between church and non-church persons create a one-way and ultimately toxic kind of evangelism. By evangelism, we refer to the ways that churches tend to relate to those who are poor and unchurched.

> **Sharp distinctions between church and non-church persons create a one-way and ultimately toxic kind of evangelism.**

In Eltham and Kidbrooke the church community is very small, while the numbers of the poor, socially excluded and educationally deprived are significantly larger. In the midst of this the church positions itself as the giver, the source or the patron of good news, or of some kind of blessings that the significant majority must take hold of. This is compounded by the fact that, usually, those outside the church can more easily feel labelled and stigmatized: mental health challenges, poverty and deprivation, joblessness, domestic violence, drug use, and so on. They cannot imagine that they could belong to a community that seems so much more socially acceptable than they are: the church, unlike Jesus, appears not to be the friend of sinners and outcasts, even though its members are in fact caring and, to some extent, are from the estate and have experienced some of the same issues to one degree or another. The sacred walls of the church give an impression of being designed to enfold the respectable and exclude the very kinds of people to whom Jesus gave most of his attention.

What is worse is the distorted form of Christian holiness inherent in some forms of evangelism, which requires appropriate behaviour as a condition for membership and acceptance. In contrast, the first quality of Jesus' holiness was unconditional overwhelming love: love that accepted people as they were and empowered them to see their true worth and to change and become their true selves – as Zacchaeus and Matthew Levi demonstrated[6] – rather than being conditional on repentance and conformity.

Communicating the gospel in this context, where moral, institutional, religious and spiritual knowledge and power appear to reside with the few within the church, often leaves the majority on the estates feeling like outsiders. Their experience of church, perhaps at baptisms or funerals (none could afford a church wedding at more than £400), is of liturgical language they do not understand, or of feeling out of place in a congregation that is mainly better off than they are. From their point of view as outsiders, those within the church seem to live more respectable lives and are evidently better equipped educationally, so that they can understand church language. Fear of embarrassment and humiliation is perhaps the main experience of the unchurched poor who might venture into a standard Common Worship service. Where the church looks middle class and respectable in very deprived areas, it is bound to be suspected of judgementalism, especially if its primary evangelistic message is of the need to repent. Where the church is unable or unwilling to offer the simplest practical help in deprived communities, it is bound to be perceived at best as indifferent to their plight. The binary distinction (perceived or real) between churched and unchurched is toxic.

Where the church looks middle class and respectable in very deprived areas, it is bound to be suspected of judgementalism, especially if its primary evangelistic message is of the need to repent.

However, further reflection of how the gospel is communicated, particularly in the New Testament, reveals both a direct disruption of binary thinking and a reversal of who or what is valued before God. First, when we look carefully at the New Testament, Jesus' ministry is not an elitist, centralized and official one. He constantly comes into conflict with those who are the religious elite. An example of this is Matthew 23, where Jesus denounces the scribes and the Pharisees precisely because of their dualistic and judgemental approach to religion. Verses 13 to 15 are worth quoting here:

> But woe to you, scribes and Pharisees, hypocrites! For you lock people out of the kingdom of heaven. For you do not go in yourselves, and when others are going in, you stop them. Woe to you, scribes and Pharisees, hypocrites! For you cross sea and land to make a single convert, and you make the new convert twice as much a child of hell as yourselves.

Not only is Jesus a marginal figure who challenges centralized power, but he also draws into his movement a host of different kinds of people, including poor fishermen, women, tax collectors and sinners and Pharisees, often people who were quite at odds with each other. In fact, at the start of Jesus' ministry, his vision is declared in Nazareth:

> The Spirit of the Lord is upon me,
> because he has anointed me

to bring good news to the poor.
He has sent me to proclaim release to the captives
and recovery of sight to the blind,
to let the oppressed go free,
to proclaim the year of the Lord's favour.
(Luke 4.18–19)

Jesus doesn't just declare this ministry as someone above those who receive his message; he embodies their condition. Jesus is a poor man. Jesus becomes vulnerable. Jesus is arrested, maligned, stigmatized and crucified as a despicable criminal. Jesus dies. And Jesus is resurrected. His ministry arises out of the very conditions of the poor and the oppressed; and as the poor and the marginalized, he demonstrates selfless love and deep compassion.

A further non-binary approach is seen in the emergence of the early church. The first Council of the Church at Jerusalem recorded in Acts 11 was to consider whether non-Jewish persons could be a part of the early followers of Jesus. Just before this, the clear leader among the apostles, Peter, had to confront his perceptions of God's view of who was in the movement of the Spirit, and who was not. In Acts 10, Peter receives a dream or vision in which his deepest religious assumptions are challenged. He is challenged to kill and eat unclean animals. Peter protests and is told not to call unclean what God makes clean.

When Peter wakes, he realizes that the bigger narrative has to do with his views about Gentile followers of Jesus – people who, as far as he could see, could not be part of the new Jesus movement. What follows in the rest of Acts 10, with the conversion of Cornelius and his household, is a strategic movement of the Holy Spirit to transcend binary distinctions between Jews and Gentiles in the earliest days of the church. The Spirit moves beyond borders and boundaries and operates beyond the walls of Peter's ideas and perceptions.

There is something deeper to consider. The biblical examples above, and the clear generosity and compassion demonstrated in Eltham and Kidbrooke, challenge what we should understand the church to be. It seems that two ideas of church are present. First, the Church is seen as a 'monument'. It is the structure that reminds others of the beliefs and doctrines arising from the church's history. It makes distinctions between those who belong to the monument and its cult, and those who do not. Those who do not understand the story, the narrative and the language will continually be outsiders. Alternatively, there is an understanding of the church as 'movement'. A movement transcends boundaries and will seek to integrate diverse persons and contexts. Movements are dynamic and seek to involve new stories and narratives.

When considering the very nature of the church, inevitably challenged by ministry on estates, two biblical theologians challenge us to continually see the church's structure and mission as 'movement', not 'monument'.

First, Richard Bauckham offers a dynamic understanding of what it means to be the church and to carry out mission in our contemporary, postmodern age. In his book, *Bible and Mission: Christian Witness in a Postmodern World*, he argues that Christendom and its universalistic and imperialistic notions of church created huge problems for those who were deemed non-Christian.[7] These problems have included stigmatization, criminalization and even genocide. However, in our postmodern world, where universalistic ideas are contested, long-held assumptions about power and about centres and margins are constantly being revised. In this case, Bauckham suggests that we see the biblical narrative as an interplay between the universal and the particular. This involves movement. In fact, he suggests three movements. First, there is the temporal. God is always moving from the old to the new, to an ever-new future. Second, there is the spatial. God moves from one place to every place. God moves to ever-new horizons. Finally, there is the social. God moves from one person to all persons. God moves to inhabit an ever-new people. This concept of movement suggests that the work of the church, the work of God, is never limited to the church. Actually, the very notion of the church should never be static.

Second, Old Testament theologian, Walter Brueggemann, surveys the prophetic tradition within Scripture, and ultimately in the life of Jesus, to trace two kinds of consciousness that inform the contemporary church. In *The Prophetic Imagination*, Brueggemann makes a distinction between Royal Consciousness and Prophetic Consciousness.[8] Royal Consciousness is the convergence of centralized power, temple cult and kingdom mindset as evidenced in the political and theological dynamics of the Hebrew Bible. For example, with the move from the rule of judges to the rule of kings, there is a fundamental shift to having a leadership like the other 'nations'. There is also a shift from worshipping and encountering God in the tent of meeting, to the construction of the temple. Essentially, there is a shift from theocratic to monarchical rulership. Alternatively, Prophetic Consciousness arises to protest against Royal Consciousness. With the rise of the kings, prophets emerge from the margins to challenge kingly power. They are often quite odd and ambivalent individuals whose power cannot be controlled by the machinations of the state. We see this in the contests between Elijah and Jezebel, for example (1 Kings 19). The theological significance of their work is their insistence that God is still a tabernacle God whose movement and presence cannot be contained within a temple; who cares for the vulnerable and the marginalized; who resists exploitation of all kinds; and, ultimately, who does what Royal Consciousness cannot – brings new life.

Brueggemann traces these dynamics in the life of Jesus, who is the epitome of Prophetic Consciousness. He mourns with the sick and dying; he includes the stigmatized and marginalized; he brings hope to the hopeless; he exposes the numbness of imperial power and false religion; he does not fear death. Ultimately, Jesus does what Caesar cannot: he rises from the dead! For Brueggemann, the true power of the church is having this kind of dynamic Prophetic Consciousness that crosses all boundaries and contests every false power, including historic and classic conceptions of church.

The true power of the church is having this kind of dynamic Prophetic Consciousness that crosses all boundaries and contests every false power, including historic and classic conceptions of church.

The limits of being Christian

Two things become very clear when considering Eltham and Kidbrooke. First, Christian ministry is very hard, since the way such ministry is packaged and dispensed is often seen as imposing and strange to the impoverished majority. Second, it is undeniable that there is a deep spirituality among those outside the walls of the church, a spirituality grounded in deep compassion and generosity. Persons who do not come to church, or who refuse to adopt the cult and culture of the church on the estate, live in ways more consistent with Jesus' movement of kenotic love. This brings us to what seems to be an ultimate question that this chapter cannot solve, but can only consider: 'What is the limit of being Christian?'

To elaborate, there is something about how we have framed Christianity and the Christian person that we need to look at again. For example, is the Christian person someone who primary believes a set of doctrines; or someone in relationship with a God who comes to us in Christ, sustains us through the Spirit, but remains beyond all doctrinal conceptions? On estates, churches provide clear boundaries to delineate between those who are members and those who are not. Examples of these might be those who are baptized or confirmed, or those who pay tithes, or those who assent to particular creedal statements, or those who are heads of ministries. To those outside such boundaries, being Christian looks more like membership of a very exclusive group.

Yet Jesus seems to defy this kind of simplistic notion of being his follower. His movement includes women, disgraced persons, marginal persons and definite outsiders to the religious elite of his day. One striking scene from Jesus' ministry is the cleansing of the temple in Matthew 21.12–17, where, after driving out those selling and buying in the temple, he declares it to be a place of prayer. However, what is particularly striking is what follows. He invites the blind and the lame into the temple and cures them. He restores the temple to its fundamental purpose. Similarly, the framing of Christianity in terms of institutional membership seems to do a disservice to what it means to be Christian in the first place.

It is this reconceptualizing of what it means to be Christian that we encourage. While ministry on estates often has a definite sense of being church, usually in a 'monument' sense of the word, we encourage a new sense of being Christian in the 'movement' sense of the word. The original term for the early disciples was not 'Christian', but 'Followers of the Way'.[9] The very terminology involved movement, relationship and mutual encounter. Centuries of Christendom has influenced the term 'Christian' to signify someone who adheres to a body of beliefs or cultic practices primarily, usually of a particular church or denomination. Followers of the Way, or disciples, signifies persons who are connected to and in relationship with a person, moving in a particular direction, being transformed in the process.

Ministry on estates like Eltham and Kidbrooke challenges the traditional idea of being Christian, since among those outside the church, one often finds what can only be described as Followers of the Way. They live and love in a way reminiscent of the early disciples, particularly in their boundless generosity and compassion. In fact, they often have no problem with believing in Jesus, or respecting Scripture. What they often reject, more than anything else, are the presumptions and judgements of the church! From our point of view, any kind of ministry on estates, or Christian ministry in general, should rediscover the relational, dynamic, transformative and love-filled understanding of Followers of the Way, and keep this as the primary means of engagement. Becoming a member of the church, which includes knowing the language, creeds and cultic practices, is important. Yes. But this is a secondary means of engagement. It should come not to evangelize persons, but to help deepen their already committed participation in the movement of Jesus.

> Among those outside the church, one often finds what can only be described as Followers of the Way. They live and love in a way reminiscent of the early disciples, particularly in their boundless generosity and compassion.

Conclusion

Eltham and Kidbrooke continues to be a deeply challenging place for Christian ministry. However, it also continues to be a site for witnessing the beauty and grace of God in the most unexpected places and among the most unexpected persons. It challenges us to think carefully about what it means to be Christian, and who can be called Christian. Perhaps we, within our orthodox ways of thinking and believing, must get back to the notion of 'disciples' and 'pilgrims', which capture this moving, dynamic relationship that is more powerful than doctrinal precision. Ultimately, we within the Christian faith must wrestle with a God who is both immanent and transcendent. The Holy Spirit works within both the church and the world. In fact, can there be a realistic boundary between the two? While we have paid attention to a movement in the church or churches, we have failed to pay attention to all the ways in which renewal and revival are taking place outside its walls. Nick and his team from Eltham and Kidbrooke sum it up this way:

> As the people of Israel journeyed through the desert (and as the community of disciples worked with Jesus), they were transformed. The people of Israel were healed of the appalling damage done by their slavery. They grew spiritually. But they also continued to be a work in progress. Being blessed by and belonging to the healing and transforming missional community unconditionally is our principle. It is also the Christians who learn from the non-Christians, who are valued for what they can contribute as well as for who they are – precious children of God. Christian belief and Christian behaviour grow out of that rather than being a prerequisite.

6

Durrington: The place of beauty

BEN EADON AND JAMES HAWKEY

What was once a sparsely populated rural location and home to nurseries, mostly known for producing tomatoes, has become an area in which more than 15,000 people now live and is essentially a suburb of Worthing. The parish is primarily residential and has a diversity of housing, of which roughly one-fifth are households living in local-authority or housing-association properties. There is a wide range of economic backgrounds and, according to the Church Urban Fund, its deprivation ranking is 3,668 out of 12,382 parishes.[1]

While Durrington is categorized as an 'estate parish', it would probably not be considered as such by many of its residents. This is in part owing to the fact that there is no housing estate of a significant size in Durrington. However, there are many small estates across the parish, a number of which were built, along with other private housing, in the 1960s and 1970s. Development continues in a limited way in a town that is hemmed in by the sea to the south, the South Downs to the north and already populous areas both on the east and west sides. In the west of the parish a further development is currently being built, which will consist of about 700 homes and include some affordable housing.

The parish is served by three primary schools as well as some small shops, pubs, a Tesco Extra, a library, a health centre, a further education college, a hospice, a gym, civic services, several community centres and three church communities, among other organizations and services. Buses provide public transport in and out of the centre of town.

Durrington presents, in many ways, as a pleasant but unexciting place. However, it only takes a bit of a scratch to discover beneath the surface some issues of concern present in the community. There have been a few stabbings in recent years as well as low-level antisocial behaviour, and there is a low level of gang culture together with county lines increasingly affecting the area. The impact of this has resulted in young people from the community being targeted and recruited into organized crime. This is particularly worrying for a local high school that borders the parish and has recently written to parents, along with some other local secondary schools that have also written to parents, to ask them to check their children's bags and coats as well as keep tabs on their whereabouts.

Equally concerning is the poverty, most of it hidden, that exists in the community. Anecdotal evidence provides glimpses of homes in which nutrition is so poor that some children present in school with severe cases of constipation or incontinence and for whom a free school lunch is the only option of a nutritious meal. Unemployment plunges some families into high levels of deprivation, while for others, working patterns negatively affect family life. It is not uncommon for parents to have two or more jobs in order to cover the bills owing to low wages or the unemployment of the other parent. In some two-parent families, time spent together can be in short supply because, in order to be present to look after the children, one parent may work night shifts while the other works day shifts. Other areas of concern include a lack of boundaries about appropriate language and topics of conversation when children are present.

Through time spent listening to members of the community in a variety of settings, themes that have surfaced in the local area include the dreams and aspirations of children, what the sense of community is like, challenges in daily life and a sense of pressure to conform. However, the theme that has been present in nearly every conversation is the place and value of beauty. The term 'housing estate' possibly doesn't conjure up thoughts of beauty, and it would be fair to say that much of the housing in Durrington would not be considered beautiful by a majority of people. But in many conversations, residents placed value on and gave insights into the décor of their home, as well as items that they collect and the importance of beauty in nature and other places.

The snapshots that follow do not use real names, but they do give accounts of real conversations. It should be noted, though, that in writing up these conversations, one loses a certain sense of the colour and vitality of the encounters.

Karen sometimes receives verbal abuse during her daily routine of walking around Durrington on account of the way she looks. This has had an effect on her depression and anxiety with which she suffers. Karen speaks about the importance of educating people about living with difference and the need for kindness. In spite of this, she also values the community in which she lives and finds people are, on the whole, friendly. She takes much pride in her garden and her collection of rose bushes. The garden is a place where she finds tranquillity and values the beauty of her roses. She also collects (some might say hoards) various mechanical objects, but owing to the modest size of her home, she has to cull her collection every so often – something with which she struggles.

Sonia works at the local supermarket and loves the opportunity her job gives for talking with people in the community. It was interesting to note how much she cares about the appearance of her home. When we met, she requested to meet at the vicarage as she didn't feel her home was presentable that day. She spoke positively of life in Durrington and of a sense of community, although she is concerned by the numbers of people she encounters who live with mental health issues. She lives within a unit of high-density housing, and she spoke of the impact the antisocial behaviour of her neighbours has on her daily life – enough to cause insomnia, nightmares and depression. She shared her frustrations about the housing association, who often seem unresponsive, especially when disputes arise between neighbours. Sonia also spoke about the many positives she perceives about Durrington, including the growth in numbers of immigrants and the subsequent increase in the diversity of people in the community. Central to Sonia's well-being are her pets (dogs and birds), and she spoke of her love of gardening, talking about how her garden is a place of beauty and somewhere she finds a sense of calm.

Jenny spoke to us about the significant sacrifices she has made in her working life in order to look after her children. She works night shifts on a part-time basis and her partner works during the day. She dislikes the aesthetics of the estate on which she lives and has had problems with her neighbours' antisocial behaviour, which includes fighting and noise, often fuelled by binge drinking. She has concerns about her children's exposure to this behaviour and the influence it has on them. In addition to her family, she places significance on the existence of her pets (cats and reptiles) and values her collection of posters of blockbuster films. She has collected the posters over a number of years, and when asked about their importance, she spoke about memories associated with seeing the films as well as her appreciation of them as artwork.

John and Joanne have three young children, including one with a severe health condition. John has lived in Durrington his entire life. They spoke about the sense of community that exists and how it is particularly evident when there is a crisis. In order to look after their child, who needs constant support, John had to give up a skilled job in order to take up an unskilled and lower-paid job which has given him a more flexible work pattern. They spoke about their experience of living in Durrington and about concerns regarding the dangers in the community, which included a stabbing on their street as well as a very obvious presence of drug dealing taking place on street corners near to their house. In order to avoid difficulties, they don't instigate any kind of contact with the drug dealers when passing them, and John, who enjoys doing maintenance on his car, does this at his mother's house rather than his own. However, they don't allow these experiences to colour their overall experience of the community. In terms of priorities and joy in their lives, they spoke about enjoying spending time in each other's company and how valuable time is spent together as a family. Again, the garden and the importance of outdoor space was mentioned.

In other conversations that were had, sometimes within a group or second-hand from members of the community, negative themes shared included the issue of poverty. Issues included high levels of anxiety among children, the effects of violence and aggression, and an unwillingness to go outside Durrington (for example, some children have never been taken to the beach in Worthing by their family and only visit it for the first time when they go on a school trip). As an example, one young girl can give a vibrant description of her make-up collection and all the different products she has, what colours they are and how she wants to be a beautician. Sadly, the reality is that she has none of these things and she sleeps in a bed with no duvet and no sheets. It's as if this rich imagination allows her to cope with the absence of basic necessities.

Despite a number of fears and anxieties being shared in the conversations, it would be wrong to go away with the perception that people live predominantly unhappy or miserable lives in Durrington. It's clear and should be reflected that most people express a sense of pride in their living environment and also in their community. On the whole, people feel a sense of community and friendliness among their immediate neighbours. However, where there are exceptions these often have a significant impact on quality of life, and where there are disruptions or problems with other groups or individuals, the most common strategy appears to be to avoid the person or group of people.

The resourcefulness and resilience where people are living with deeply imbedded concerns should also be recognized. Whenever anyone spoke about an issue that has a negative impact on their life, they tended to counter it with something that is good and positive in their life. Most significantly, people generally commented on something that was not just positive but beautiful in their life, whether something that they do, something they collect or something they have created.

Gardens were mentioned frequently, either as a point of connection among neighbours, a general pastime or in terms of appreciating nature and beauty, along with the importance for many of keeping pets. Collections of items regarded as precious to the owner were often shown during visits. They might well be items that would not generally be considered beautiful and probably have little monetary value, but they are regarded by their owner as precious and demonstrate the capacity to see beauty in even quite ordinary objects. When talking with children, a sense of beauty was often palpable when they spoke about their dreams and aspirations in terms of what they wanted to do and what they wanted to have. Among the children, there was also a clear emphasis placed on their ability to create beauty, whether through physical means or imagination.

In terms of deprivation, one so often thinks about need and necessity in terms of having a place to live, having enough money or having access to shops, healthcare, education and other services. The experience of this listening project has demonstrated that beauty, however it is found or perceived, is not an optional extra, but a requirement for a person's flourishing. It may seem surplus to requirements or extravagant, but what has emerged from conversations in Durrington is that beauty is a basic human need. If the mainstream view is that beauty makes little difference to quality of life, such as not worrying about what a building looks like so long as it provides a basic need, then we need to think again. It's hardly surprising that the normal reaction of a class of schoolchildren entering a church is to immediately look around with a sense of amazement – they stop to look at the sense of space, the colour of stained glass and other decorative features. Perhaps we need to rethink what it is to be human, to allow for the importance that beauty plays in each of our lives.

> **Beauty, however it is found or perceived, is not an optional extra, but a requirement for a person's flourishing.**

'The dearest freshness deep down things':[2] a meditation on beauty and theology

JAMES HAWKEY

Christian thinkers need to deploy a considerable degree of care when thinking about beauty, especially when considering what aesthetic categories make something or someone beautiful. "'Beauty is truth, truth beauty" – that is all ye know on earth, and all ye need to know', wrote Keats at the end of 'Ode on a Grecian Urn'.[3] And yet, Christian concepts of the beautiful are more complex than this, especially when they are linked to questions of truth or revelation. Jesus Christ – the *icon* 'of the invisible God, the firstborn of all creation' (Col. 1.15) and source of beauty in all things living – reveals his ultimate truth to the human race as he is publicly disfigured on a rough instrument of torture and execution. Celebrating the cross as the most iconic image of Christian worship, the sixth-century hymn-writer Venantius Fortunatus could speak of it in terms which, at a surface level, appear contradictory and, frankly, bizarre:

O Tree of beauty, Tree of light,
O Tree with royal purple dight,
Elect on whose triumphal breast
Those holy limbs should find their rest.[4]

That which is gruesome and shocking is described as radiant and consoling. There is a paradoxical yet innate beauty here, because of what is actually going on within the scene itself. This is certainly not a 'surface' beauty, but when seen in the light of the deep truth of the passion of the Son of God, it can be both described and portrayed as beautiful, lustrous and life-giving.

It's important to pause for a moment and consider both these moves: described *and* portrayed. A verbal description of the crucifixion as something beautiful activates the imagination. In other words, it registers in the realm of the pictorial. It is possible for an artist to tell a very deep truth without being imprisoned by attempting to portray the details of the original scene. Art and poetry are acts of faith, expressions of love and offerings of worship, rather than simple straightforward reportage. While this may particularly be the case for religious artists, it can also be so for those who are often described as secular artists. The hazy effects deployed by the French impressionists, for example, are not designed to obscure reality, but rather to reveal it in a fuller way, and to offer a richer insight into those otherwise day-to-day, seemingly mundane scenes.

One of my most treasured possessions is a cross made for me by a young person in my former parish, in inner-city Portsmouth. Five lollipop sticks, painted green and orange, are held together by lumps of sticky tape. It's thin and fragile, but it represents the faith and creativity of someone who lived a disturbed and unstable life in our parish and who found peace in church in the midst of a shattered and dangerous home situation. This cross speaks to me of a deep hope in the love of the crucified and a hallowing of the everyday, using waste material to express the beauty of Christian truth. Part of its beauty is in the fact that it was made by someone whose story I was privileged to know, and who struggled with the contradictions and demands of human life and faith.

The act of *making* is itself one of profound importance. It represents a sharing in the creativity of God who is Trinity. Those who visited Durrington for this listening project reported pride not only in the beauty of gardens and flowers, but also in the role that human creativity – spontaneous or otherwise – plays in this community. The scrawling of colourful pictures on a bedroom wall by a child

> The act of *making* is one that seeks liberation and truth. It reminds us both of our own human agency and of our participation in the freedom of God himself.

who has difficulty speaking, the rich imagination of another child who doesn't even own a duvet, or the obsession of a young person with sharing the vibrant colours of her make-up kit, all speak a language of beauty, an aesthetic which reveals a creative longing for that which is beyond the immediate. Surely, here as everywhere, there is a sense of beauty as being something conditioned and shaped by culture and environment, but the *act* of making is one that seeks liberation and truth. It reminds us both of our own human agency and of our participation in the freedom of God himself.

The romantic critic John Ruskin believed that the work of an artisan resembled God's own work, as 'free, creative, delighting in its creation'.[5] Similarly, acts of free, expressive creativity place the mundanity of the present moment within a much wider context, where the future is open to co-creation, and where the boundaries of the possible stretch out in hope and potential. Paying attention to such creativity in the life of the home or the school is to recognize dignity and encourage growth. The Jewish composer Viktor Ullmann composed a large number of works while imprisoned in Theresienstadt concentration camp. He was asked how he could compose under prison circumstances. His response was that these conditions actually helped him, because 'the will to create is the same as the will to live'.[6]

It is often said colloquially that beauty is 'in the eye of the beholder'. Many gallons of ink have been spilt over whether it is ever possible to discuss beauty in anything approaching absolute terms. Our opening thoughts about the aesthetic categories that can be deployed in describing or portraying the crucifixion perhaps make any straightforward statements about how form or balance, for example, might contribute any essential 'ingredient' for an assessment of beauty pretty tricky.

We've briefly considered the act of *making* – the expressive mode – but what about the act of pondering, gazing or contemplating something? The philosopher Douglas Hedley poses the question rhetorically: 'Is the world just the backdrop for human interests or locus of the breakthrough of the Kingdom of God?'[7]

The imagination not only allows us to transcend the ordinary; it also enables us to become witnesses of a new creation that is promised. Jesus teaches that it is not possible to receive the kingdom of God unless we become like children (Matt. 18.3). A refreshed capacity for imagination and playful wonder, perhaps especially when considering that which the world considers mundane, is one of the marks of a truly free person. We frequently learn from those who are very young, in whom the reflex of wonder is often so fresh. Beauty is something we see and experience – it is subjective – but this is a response to the sheer objectivity of what is given. Our experience of delight is one of recognition of that which *is*.

The imagination not only allows us to transcend the ordinary; it also enables us to become witnesses of a new creation that is promised.

One of the theological reasons why this matters so profoundly is linked to what we believe about grace. Both the imagination and a straightforward appreciation of nature and creativity are fed by the creeping insistence that creation is something abundant, and held in being by the One who is infinite and eternally creative. The capacity for God's work is limitless gift, and the resurrection – the ultimate and final transgression of boundaries – invites our participation in that work as an act of witness.

The natural world is not beautiful primarily because it is useful or functional. It is beautiful because its gratuitous superfluity is a sign of the infinite. We should be suspicious of our own creations when they are solely praised for reasons of utility or function. There are implications here for housing policy, design and town planning, as well as for church architecture, liturgy and parish life. School curricula and youth group programmes that encourage creativity and cultivate attention will contribute both to social harmony and the spiritual and emotional development of the young people they help to form. A renewed public focus on the environment, and the urgent need to see human beings as an organic part of nature rather than separate from it, may help us regain our sight. We recognize the beautiful in all its diverse shapes and forms, because it moves us more deeply into the truth.

The Jesuit poet Gerard Manley Hopkins wrote, 'The world is charged with the grandeur of God',[8] and that despite humanity's abuse of the earth, its insistence on industry and, we might add, the supreme irony of a mass-producing yet throwaway culture, its inherent beauty is untarnished. There is, he tells us, the 'dearest freshness deep down things'.[9] This 'dearest freshness' is a quality of givenness which we sense as much in the free doodles of a child as in the simple beauty of a flower. It also encourages us to face that which can be terrifying or destabilizing – in other words, this 'dearest freshness' is present even in situations of pain or horror, which we might be tempted to ignore, or from which we would rather look away. The twelfth-century mystic, Richard of St Victor, perceived *ubi amor, ibi oculus*: 'where there is love, there is seeing'.[10] We must respond to what is before us and, in the depths of that reality, recognize Christ.

How we look at the world, how our imagination is fed and how our eyes might recognize intrinsic beauty – that 'dearest freshness deep down things' – in the whole of creation is a deeply Christian question, because it relates to Christ, the Wisdom and Word of the Father, the agent of creation and the one whose death and resurrection have opened the new creation for us. A residual fear of idolatry and an over-developed sense of the transcendent otherness of God at the expense of God's creative immanence have frequently made western Christians nervous of seeking God 'in all things'. Yet, this is the earlier tradition – redemption as a cosmic event, the resurrection itself a renewal of nature. This is the beauty our eyes long to see; a beauty recognized in the imagination, as well as in the freshness deep down in ordinary things.

The French orthodox emigré Olivier Clément put it like this:

> To save ourselves we must give up all security, any notion of being self-sufficient; we must look at the world with wonder, gratefully receiving it anew, with its mysterious promise of the infinite. Everything – the world, history, other people

and myself – can be a source of revelation, because through everything we can discern, like a watermark, the face of the Risen Christ, the Friend who secretly shares with each of us the bread of affliction and the wine of mirth.[11]

7

Listening for good news: Reflections on the process

AL BARRETT

The project is not about coming up with a single, formulaic answer to the question, 'What is the good news for the estates?' Rather it is about developing a transferable theological method in which our proclamation is based on a deep listening to the issues that estates residents are thinking, caring and worrying about. This is deeply rooted in commitment to an incarnational, transformative praxis.
(Bishop Philip North, Estates Theology Project proposal document, 2017)

This was how Bishop Philip described the project when it was still just the seed of an idea. It has grown and developed in various ways since then – and I'll try to describe some of those developments below. Maybe 'a transferable theological method' was over-ambitious – we'll see – but the core of that idea remains: this project, and what we want to offer from its fruit, has been about all kinds of fascinating 'whats?' (I hope you agree that the preceding chapters have been rich with nourishing, challenging content) – but as much, if not more, about the 'how?'.

So how did we do what we did? At its simplest:

- we found a place;
- we found some people;
- we listened.

There was more to it than that, of course. But it's worth stating like that, because often what *sounds* obvious may not necessarily be what commonly happens. In what follows, we'll dig into each of these in more depth, noting some of the complexities and knotty questions along the way.

Place

Estates vary widely, and there is no one, universally agreed definition of what counts as an 'estate'. We *don't* mean the expansive grounds of a medieval manor house (although if you look up 'estate' in the dictionary, that's one option you'll find. We're *not*, in this work, focused on new-build commuter-belt areas (although attention to those is an important, if distinct, piece of work). The kind of estates we *are* talking about are often defined by a high proportion of social housing (and often, as a consequence, high levels of economic deprivation, or 'suppressed abundance' as I reframed it earlier). These are often found, geographically, on the outer edges of our cities – but not only in those places. Their residents might often be characterized as – and often name themselves as – 'working class', although analysis of class divisions has been complexified in recent decades, and it should be stated here, lest we forget, that whatever we mean by 'working class', it cannot just mean 'White'. In the Great British Class Survey of 2011, of those counted as 'emergent service workers' or 'precariat', 21 per cent and 13 per cent respectively were people of global majority heritage.[1]

A further characteristic common to many estates (but again, not all) was a sense of clear geographical boundedness (lines that define whether you're either 'on the estate' or 'not on the estate') – something that, as writer Lynsey Hanley has described, often profoundly shapes estate-dwellers psychologically: the 'wall in the head'.[2] This factor particularly, often alongside low levels of car ownership and poor public transport infrastructure, means that *paying attention to the place* is of vital importance in estate neighbourhoods. *Being present* in the neighbourhood, talking to 'the locals' (whether they've lived there for sixty years or six weeks)

Paying attention to the place is of vital importance in estate neighbourhoods. Being present ... and talking about the place – all of these were critical in our project.

and talking *about* the place – all of these were critical in our project. We were also keen to get a good geographical spread of places, including the estates in and around the cities of London (Eltham), Birmingham (Rubery), Manchester (Wythenshawe) and Newcastle (Cowgate), as well as two non-urban estates in Kent (Twydall) and Wiltshire (Durrington).

People

At the heart of the project was the conviction that *bringing into conversation people from different locations enables us to see more, and differently.* Wherever we

At the heart of the project was the conviction that *bringing into conversation people from different locations enables us to see more, and differently.*

are located (both geographically and within the nexus of other factors that make up our personal identities), there are some things that we are able to see clearly and some things of which we are oblivious.[3] We need the perceptions and insights of others, located differently, to help us get a fuller, richer, clearer picture of reality.

This conviction was behind the bringing together of locally rooted practitioners and theologians based in academic contexts. What might the academic see and hear in the estate that those of us who are estates practitioners (for whom it is the air that we breathe, the sea in which we swim every day) might not be noticing? What generative insights for theological reflection might perhaps be taken for granted by the practitioner, but startling and challenging for the academic? What might they learn from each other's contexts and areas of expertise?

But more than that – the core work of the project was listening not to the practitioner or the academic, but to the local residents of the estates, both those who counted themselves as part of 'church' and those who didn't. It was *their* experiences, longings, insights and convictions that we were most interested in hearing, and in being challenged and changed by. We'll explore more of that process of listening in the next section.

We should note here that the temptation to 'othering' (to refer to a 'them' who, by definition, are different from 'us'), with its associated tendency to make sweeping generalizations (whether positive, negative or neutral), was something we were sharply conscious of, and keen to do our best to avoid. We should also note here some of the limits to the diversity of our own group (of practitioners and academics): we were significantly male heavy, almost all White, and had few people from working-class backgrounds among our number. While in many ways these failings reflect wider structural issues in both academic theology and the Church of England, we remain conscious of the ways they have limited the insights of the project – and of some of the ways in which, if we were to do something similar again, we could do better.

Listening

This brings us to the practicalities, the purpose and the politics of listening. Bishop Philip's original proposal for this project started with a description of the praxis of Jesus: 'He sought to understand an individual before he proclaimed the Good News in a way that answered their questions and made sense to their lives.'[4]

If Jesus is the one person who most fully 'meets our deepest needs', he continued, then it is vital in our evangelism to get to know *who people are*, and to better hear and understand 'the issues impacting on the[ir] lives'. Frustratingly, he argued, 'the background of our clergy, the expectations of the church, and the nature of our theological establishment' make that hearing and understanding more difficult. And as a result, 'we are all too often offering articulate answers but to the wrong questions', and thus 'impoverishing' our witness to Jesus Christ.[5]

As we set to work as a group, engaging with each other and with the people in the six estate neighbourhoods, it's fair to say that this initial way of setting up the idea of 'listening deeply' came under increasing scrutiny and critique. Were we really listening, primarily, for local people's 'questions', so that we could then come up with more contextually appropriate 'answers'? Or was something more open-ended, and perhaps deeper, going on?

In at least some of the parishes involved in this project, the listeners decided to ask something like these three questions (as in Chapter 1):

1 What do you love about this place?
2 What gives you grief here?
3 What can the church be for you here?

It *is* possible to hear in the framing of those questions the beginnings of a response – especially in the third. But the first two were deliberately expressed to be as open as possible, to invite the person to share something of themselves and the texture of their life-in-this-place, without being narrowed into multiple choice answers or pre-determined themes. As we engaged in listening, we glimpsed something of its positive power *as an end in itself*. As one member of the group observed, 'People have so many stories – and nowhere safe to tell them'.

'People have so many stories – and nowhere safe to tell them'.

Another reported back the words of a participant in one of the listening exercises, which was said with surprise and gratitude: 'Someone from outside [the estate] listened to me!'

At one of our group sessions, in June 2018, we invited Andrew Grinnell, coordinator of the network of Poverty Truth Commissions that have been set up around the UK, to help us think through *how* we were listening and *why*. Andrew pointed us to the work of Otto Scharmer, who distinguishes between four different 'levels' of listening:[6]

- 'Downloading' – where we take in what we hear only so far as it reconfirms our pre-existing opinions and judgements: 'I knew you'd say that.'
- 'Factual listening' – where we notice some of the differences between what we're hearing and what we already knew: 'I've learnt something here.'
- 'Empathic listening' – where our listening enables us to deepen an emotional connection, helping us see something of life through the other person's eyes: 'I feel something of what you're going through.'
- 'Generative listening' – which nurtures a space between the listener and the listened-to and allows something new or unexpected to emerge, which transforms both of us: 'Something surprising has happened here and we've both been changed by it.'

How we approach opportunities to listen, then, makes all the difference. Do our listening encounters, at one extreme, simply confirm the rightness of everything we believe and are doing already? Or, at the other extreme, do they reveal the language, categories and practices of our Christian faith to be utterly 'bust'? At times within our group, members articulated something of both extremes – and plenty more of our conversations fell into various locations between those two. Our positions were, we acknowledged, significantly shaped by our differing understandings of mission, evangelism and 'witness' (we'll return to this question shortly), but also by the differences in our established relationships with our neighbours, and our attentiveness to *power*.

We found – perhaps unsurprisingly – that being able to move into serious, generative listening to local people, especially those beyond the boundaries of 'church', often depended on pre-existing relationships of trust between the local practitioner and individuals or groups. The extent of such relationships varied quite widely within our group, dependent not just on the length of time someone had been working in their particular context, but also on the approach they had taken to ministry there. For some in our group, this was the first time they had done some relatively intensive, intentional listening to parishioners beyond their church congregation. This varied extent of local relationships of trust highlighted one of the initial premises of this project: that there is, indeed, often a disconnection between local churches and their neighbours. We came to frame this as a trust problem that worked both ways: local people may not trust people from 'the church', but the local church may also often have not made itself vulnerable enough to 'entrust' its neighbours.

Local people may not trust people from 'the church', but the local church may also often have not made itself vulnerable enough to 'entrust' its neighbours.

As the project developed, many members of the group expressed concerns – or a certain intentional 'vigilance' – around the 'politics' of our listening. Such a concern was right and proper. Listening, like any interpersonal interaction, involves an exercise of power – and also (with the kind of questions we were asking) an invitation into various kinds of vulnerability. Among our forms of vigilance, then, were:

- a desire to protect and nurture fledgling and fragile relationships locally, and not to do anything that might risk exploiting them, damaging them or stretching them further than they were currently ready for;
- a proper caution about sharing more widely the personal stories of others – even with their informed consent;
- a concern to avoid 'othering' or objectifying those we listened to – draining the life and detail from a story in its retelling, holding it up as representative of 'estate people' in general, or exoticizing or romanticizing it as a curiosity from a context very different from our own;
- a warning (from local residents) for us to not come away from our listening with neat, know-it-all analysis – to acknowledge the complexity of, and everything that we *don't* know about, people and their lives;
- a resistance to presenting ourselves as Good Samaritans, saviours

or helpers, and those we listen to as needy, lacking or victims, in ways that are paternalistic or patronizing, and which only serve to reinforce imbalances of power in our relationships.

How we listened to local people, then, was entangled with questions of *why* we were listening to them. In our sharing together as a group – always friendly and curious, but also sometimes heated with passion and the frustrations of disagreement and speaking past each other – gradually our differing understandings of the purpose of the project began to emerge, often rooted in our differing understandings of mission, evangelism and witness.

Purpose, missiologies and models of 'witness'

Why were we seeking to engage with local people in estate neighbourhoods, both inside and outside church? Underneath that question lay a deeper one: 'Why does the local church engage with its neighbours at all?' In our conversations together, *prepositions* became significant. So often these little words look like minor details in a sentence, but different prepositions configure our relationships differently. In our case, which preposition we used had a profound effect on how we imagined and embodied the threefold relationships between:

- the local church;
- its estate-resident neighbours;
- and ourselves as a group (part of the wider church).

In what follows, I outline four different configurations of those relationships, based on four different prepositions. All four configurations, and understandings of 'witness',[7] were present in our small group, pushing and pulling at each other for centrality in our work. And while we had to make some decisions about *what* we did, *how* we did it and *why*, even in this final chapter of the project's journey there remains a certain amount of unavoidable tension

– creative, at its best – that of course reflects the way in which these questions remain unresolved in the life of the church more widely.

1. For: 'reshaping our evangelism for outer estate residents'

This first model is where the project began. Our original research question was, 'What is the good news *for* estates?' This was premised on a missiology that understands Christian witness as *service* ('meeting human needs with love') and *proclamation* ('answering the questions people are asking, with a retelling of the gospel') – a movement *outwards* from church into the neighbourhood (and perhaps also from the institutional 'centre' to the estate-based 'edges' of church).

Key outcomes in this model would be *content* (resources) and a *process* (method) for evangelism that are tried and tested in outer estates – something that can be shown to be truly good news for our outer estate neighbours. The outcome for local *relationships* would therefore be largely about neighbours being willing recipients of this new and improved 'offer' from the local church. *Institutional change*, in this model, would centre on more investment in resourcing outer-estate churches.

The research process would be one of a back-and-forth movement: from the streets of the estate to the deliberations of the Estates Theology Group (and/or the pair) and back to the estate. It would start with listening to local voices (with their informed consent), but would then shift to a second phase of reflection one step removed from those voices – identifying the practical needs and the existential questions, reflecting theologically on these, and proposing some theologically inflected responses that meet the needs and answer the questions. The final phase, returning to the estate, might test out these responses with local people, and seek local approval for any content that we wish to make public.

2. From: 'being changed by our encounters with estate residents'

A second approach might ask, 'What is the good news *from* estates?' In some ways, this mirrors the first model, but with the flow moving in the opposite direction. Taking seriously the alienation that so often exists between the church and its estate-resident neighbours (a theme running throughout our reflections thus far), the essential element of Christian witness in this model is focused on what we Christians *receive* – what we see and hear in our encounters with our neighbours and how that enriches, challenges and transforms *us*.

In terms of outcomes, *content* would primarily be in the form of our own experiences of transformation through our encounters in the research *process* – which in turn would demonstrate the value of similar kinds of listening processes in other contexts. Local *relationships* might be deepened, as neighbours know not just that they have been listened to, but that what they have shared has been received as transformative. Our testimony to the institutional church would be to resist dominant, neo-colonialist and patriarchal models of 'doing *to* or *for*' in favour of a radical receptivity to those on the edges – the genuine possibility of the church being both renewed and reformed *from the margins*, as Bishop Philip himself has often argued.

The research process, within this model, would be unavoidably slower than with the first. It would rely on a deeper kind of listening, closer to Scharmer's 'generative' level, requiring a longer journey of renouncing initiative and voice, deepening trust, practising attentive presence and being open to hearing something new, surprising and challenging. It would require also a willingness for us to give up our deeply held convictions about what the good news is and how it is best embodied – and to seek (humbly, penitentially) ways in which our imaginations, language and practices might be changed. This model also, like the first, requires a 'retreat' from the local context into the deliberative space of the Estates Theology Group, but this time for something more akin to the practice of professional supervision, where the focus is on *what has changed (and been challenged) in us*, rather than on the personal narratives of those we have encountered – which are understood as not ours to share. Nevertheless, any content we wish ultimately to be made public will want to include at least some detail of encounters in the context – for which we would need to return to seek explicit consent.

3. By: 'sharing good news stories told by estates residents'

The third approach in some ways resembles the second. The question remains, 'What is the good news *from* estates?', but in this model the emphasis is on the voices of local people speaking for themselves. In some ways, this is the simplest option methodologically, as it removes from the process the mediating step of theological reflection (which might also be its critical flaw). Here, we simply ask local people, 'What is good news here?' and allow them to interpret it however they like – *their* testimony is the witness here – in their own words.

Rather than seeking estate-focused 'problems' for us Christians to 'solve', what we are likely to discover is all kinds of things that we are invited to celebrate, or join in with, or even sometimes hear as challenge to us both locally and nationally. What if (dare we imagine?) community life *beyond* the church turns out to be richer and more fulfilling than that *within* the church?! Far from being a crude Pollyanna-ish 'glass-half-full' mentality that ignores the struggles and the pressures, what we hear may well include much that is about survival – even flourishing – in the face of real adversity. Our role as listener and potentially celebrant (or cheerleader!) may well have a positive effect on our local relationships – particularly if we have been more accustomed, historically, to seeking out people's tales of woe, suffering and need.

4. With: 'discovering the good news together'

A final model emphasizes the co-production of knowledge. Guided by the Poverty Truth Commission mantra of 'nothing about us, without us, is for us',[8] it would commit us (the Estates Theology Group) to work *with* estates residents to discover the good news together. The testimony of local people is of profound value in this model, but 'witness' is something more complex simply than listening to local people talk. What is experienced here, and what can be told to others, is primarily *the journeying deeper, together, into mutually transformative relationship, and into shared discovery of the gospel.*

The primary outcome in this model, then, is stronger, more mutually trusting local *relationships.* Inevitably, this would require slowing our process down to what has been called 'the speed of trust' – especially where church–neighbourhood ties are, at present, weaker. Telling the story of the *process* itself would be one of the richest resources of this model – and those stories would be as diverse as the different contexts represented within the group. *Content* would perhaps take the most time and effort to emerge this way, but it would be content that is most securely owned by the pairs and the local residents involved in co-producing it. The learning and challenge to the *wider church* would be perhaps the most unpredictable outcome of this model – but if the process were done well, we should not underestimate the potential results.

While this model would refuse to allow us to determine the process in advance, or a 'one-size-fits-all' process across the diverse contexts represented within the group, there is nevertheless plenty of wisdom to be found among those who have embarked on similar journeys before us.

We've already mentioned the work of Poverty Truth Commissions (PTCs) around the country, where local people ('experts by experience') are brought together to meet regularly over a significant period of time and supported to grow in confidence to tell their own stories. In a second stage, this group is then introduced to decision-makers from wider institutions, whose main role is to listen and learn from the 'expert witnesses' on the Commission – with whom, as trust, friendship and challenge deepens between them, they are paired up in ongoing mentoring relationships (i.e. the local residents mentoring the decision-makers).[9]

Another well-established model is Laurie Green's account of local theological experiments in his book *Let's Do Theology.*[10] As with the PTCs, local people come together and are supported to make connections between their own stories and wider neighbourhood and societal stories – including asking 'why?' questions of the status quo (the 'analysis' phase). In a second, 'reflection', phase, the group is supported to engage with biblical texts and theological themes from their own experiences, and to read them with an eye to the liberation and flourishing of their communities. This then leads into a third phase, of the group identifying what needs to change – in their own lives and relationships, in their neighbourhoods, in wider society and in the local and wider church ('action'). In Green's model, it is most definitely the local people who *do* the theological reflection – with the role of the 'professional theologian' being more about gently supporting the process and occasionally offering some theological resources, where appropriate, for the group to draw on if they so choose.

Navigating the journey together

So where did we get to? As I've said already, even as a small group (of first six and latterly five pairs of local practitioners and academic theologians, with a handful of us alongside seeking to offer support, encouragement, challenge and some gentle coordination), significant differences emerged between us, and remained – although all of us can testify to ways in which we have learnt and been changed through our conversations together.

Much of what you have read in this book has been – as the book's subtitle suggests – 'good news *from* the estates'. A short series of podcasts, another product of this project, includes the voices and experiences of residents of three of our estate contexts, more in the 'by' mode described above. The Twydall Declaration that ends this book is a powerful example of 'with' in action (its production described in detail by Ann Richardson and Justin Stratis in their chapter). We have, on the whole, taken one or more steps back from the 'for' approach with which the project began, consciously resisting attempts to formulate answers to any questions we might have heard in our listening engagements. Nevertheless, what has emerged in our work, and has been articulated in these pages, does include a wealth of rich, locally grounded and theologically shaped insights and wonderings which, drawn on in the right contexts and in the right ways, might prove to be gifts and resources – of goodness, beauty, truth and more – for local Christians to offer to their communities, to neighbours both within and beyond the walls of the local church.

The diversity and differences of our group, our contexts, and the processes and products of our work present a gift to the wider church, then, but also remind us of a wider woundedness within the body of Christ: we Christians disagree deeply with each other on how we understand 'the gospel', 'church' and 'mission'. At its best, this project has modelled ways of listening deeply not just to our estate-dwelling neighbours, but also to each other as Christians: seeking not *resolution*, necessarily, but at the very least a deeper understanding of each other, and at best witnessing new expressions of the gospel of Jesus Christ emerging in the spaces between us.

> **At its best, this project has modelled ways of listening deeply not just to our estate-dwelling neighbours, but also to each other as Christians.**

We have also, over the four years in which we have journeyed together, witnessed profound experiences of pressure, fragility and loss. For all of us involved, in various ways, this project *has been hard to see through*. For the academics among us (especially but by no means only those employed by secular institutions), it has been at best a fringe commitment, contributing little or nothing to the Research Excellence Framework assessments that shape so much of the work of Higher Education bodies in the UK. A number of our academics moved institution mid-project and had to withdraw from their roles in this project because they felt unable to justify it to their new employer.

For local practitioners, this project may have felt more centrally important within their day-to-day ministries, but invariably it was always in competition with a list of more urgent jobs demanding their attention. Over the years of the project's duration (2017–21), parish clergy and lay leaders in the Church of England have seen a perhaps unprecedented intensification of the demands placed on them, through strategic reorganization programmes at diocesan and national levels, and the Covid pandemic which hit the UK in March 2020. While every parish has its challenges, the fragility of much of life in estate neighbourhoods (from often under-resourced churches, schools and other institutions and groups, to disproportionately high levels of mental health struggles among local people) has been felt by all involved in this project – and was perhaps the most significant factor in one of our parishes (Cowgate, Newcastle) having to withdraw from the project along the way.

We return, finally, to the Wythenshawe Weave, which framed our opening engagement with some of Jesus' parables of the kin-dom. What is offered here is no neat and tidy 'product', but diverse threads – some strong and bold, others more hidden and frayed, some that speak of woundedness and struggle, others that shine unapologetically with joy and delight – woven in ways that tell the story of the process of weaving itself: of a journey of hiddenness and finding and responding, a journey that refuses any sense of finishedness this side of God's new creation, but which, in discovering traces of good news along the way, widens our eyes, opens our ears and enlarges our hearts to search for *more* where that came from: in and among the places and people of our estate neighbourhoods, on what we are compelled to acknowledge is holy ground.

8

How can I do this where I am?

AL BARRETT AND OTHERS

As you can tell from the diversity of the chapters in this book, there is absolutely no 'one-size-fits-all' prescription for the kind of 'work' (a labour of love) we have been engaged in, in this project. But we have learnt a thing or two along the way, some rules of thumb, some dos and don'ts. We offer them here in the hope that they will encourage you to experiment where you are, to dive into your neighbourhoods afresh, with open ears and open hearts.

At its simplest . . .

1 Find a place.
2 Find some people.
3 Listen.

Some DOs to encourage you

- DO pay attention to the *place*: its boundaries, its centres, its 'bumping spaces' where people naturally hang out and/or bump into each other . . . and hang out in them!
- DO look for simple, direct signs of love and creativity at work beyond the church walls.
- DO pay attention to the *people*: find the connectors (not the same as the 'community leaders') – they will have stories to tell, and they will lead you to other storytellers!
- DO seek out local partners, local activists, local people, and

embrace their knowledge, skills and gifts – they're the experts in their local community.

- DO have an expansive ecclesiology, which takes seriously those who may seem at the fringes of the worshipping community.
- DO expect the Holy Spirit to be active in your conversations.
- DO expect to be a recipient of blessing.
- DO expect local people to have wisdom that is worth listening to – and worth sharing more widely
- DO, wherever possible, offer back what you've heard and reflected on, to those with whom you have engaged – for their revisions, vetos, questions and additions.
- DO allow space for some people to take a lead with your activity. Every community has natural leaders whose local insight and personal drive is likely to be enabled by the project you set up.
- DO allow yourself to be sidetracked at least once or twice if you have time – the peripheral conversations and issues help to sharpen your exploration of the topic at hand.

Some cautionary DON'Ts

- DON'T expect local people to be a homogenous group – expect diversity wherever you look and listen!
- DON'T get frustrated when people's answers reflect the questions they are asking rather than those you have suggested. Their response is likely to be more illuminating than your original question had allowed for.
- DON'T filter out the flippant, amusing or left-field responses, for in these can be found the joys (and sorrows) of a person's passions.
- DON'T measure success in crude metrics.
- DON'T panic! And don't try to fix it – just listen, pray and journey together.
- DON'T beat yourself up when it doesn't work, when no one turns up, when the event falls flat, when people misinterpret

good intentions, when there's a falling-out, when half the group stops talking to the other half, when the publicity arrives late or when the man at the council says 'no'. Nothing is wasted.

And if you particularly want to try a creative arts project . . .

- DO commission an artist. Not cheap, but you'll get back ten times what you pay out (and there are trust funds and community funding bodies who can help with the costs).
- DO write a brief – don't tell the artist what to make; tell them what you want them to explore, who with and why.
- DON'T worry if the outcome is transient or momentary. What you make doesn't need to last forever (and anything that's going to be permanent needs way too much paperwork!).

The Twydall Declaration

WRITTEN BY RESIDENTS OF TWYDALL, IN CONVERSATION WITH ANN RICHARDSON AND JUSTIN STRATIS

I. **We affirm** that Jesus Christ establishes the true worth and value of every person in the church. He does this not only by his sacrificial death on the cross, but also by being with us as a community, hearing our prayers, and giving each of us gifts with which to serve our fellow disciples.

We reject, therefore, a church culture which values some Christian brothers and sisters more highly than others, whether because of wealth, education, power, class or connections.

II. **We affirm** that following Christ ought to make a real difference in the way we live our lives. Christianity is a calling to follow the leading of the Lord in everything: in our work, families, friendships, communities, as well as in our political and economic life. Through the Holy Spirit, Jesus continues to direct his people, and it is our privilege and responsibility to live in the freedom of obedience to his instruction.

We reject, therefore, the reduction of Christianity to a mere religion that never leads to real change. The practices of the Christian faith are not a badge of class respectability, status, or national pride designed to exclude those of certain backgrounds; the call to genuine discipleship is open to all and reveals itself in transformed lives.

III. **We affirm** that God is with his people who live on housing estates and is already working powerfully amongst us. The kingdom of God has already come near in our midst, and this should be cause for celebration and gratitude amongst the whole people of God.

We reject the notion that social deprivation indicates God-forsakenness and its flip side that financial stability indicates God's blessing. Housing estates are not mere objects for the charity of the rich; they are diverse communities of people across the socio-economic spectrum in which the body of Christ has taken root and in which the Holy Spirit is active.

IV. **We affirm** the positive impact of clergy in our local church communities. Clergy that know and love their congregations and communities well, who speak plainly, and are faithful to God in their ministry are a gift from the Lord to us. Likewise, **we affirm** the clergy's unique position, above the fray of partisan politics, to take a stand for truth and justice in the public square, including at the highest levels of government.

Likewise, **we reject** as an abomination all past and present abuse of God's children at the hands of the clergy and regard the pursuit of justice for their victims as a gospel imperative.

V. **We affirm** the gospel's message of radical welcome and inclusion under the banner of the cross.

We reject any purportedly Christian message which unduly judges and dismisses the other for whom Christ died, whether that take the form of patriarchy, the oppression and/or neglect of the poor, homophobia, or any other exclusionary ideology.

VI. **We affirm** the beauty and diversity of the body of Christ, especially as this is manifest in the Church of England. We appreciate that people connect with God through different spiritualities and liturgical practices, and to the extent that ecclesiastical structures recognise and respond to this, they serve the body well. We are a family and so, like the parts of the body, we are absolutely inter-reliant under the headship of Christ.

We reject any arrangement of the church which fails to reflect the church's God-given diversity, seen, for instance, in the demographic uniformity of the church's leadership with respect to class, education, wealth, gender, and the like. Each Christian is a gift to the other, and so all must be heard and included as the church together seeks the mind of Christ.

Notes

Contexts and contributors

1 Al Barrett, *Interrupting the Church's Flow: A Radically Receptive Political Theology in the Urban Margins* (London: SCM Press, 2020).

2 Al Barrett and Ruth Harley, *Being Interrupted: Reimagining the Church's Mission from the Outside, In* (London: SCM Press, 2020).

1 Finding the treasure: Rooting our reflections

1 I use the term 'kin-dom' (rather than 'kingdom') here, in line with my co-writing with Ruth Harley in *Being Interrupted: Reimagining the Church's Mission from the Outside, In* (London: SCM Press, 2020). There, we explained, 'most readers will be familiar with the idea of "the kingdom of God", used by Jesus repeatedly in the Gospels. It's a term that is used deliberately, ironically, to subvert, turn on their heads, our usual understandings of "kingdoms" (hierarchical societies ruled over by a powerful monarch), and most specifically the Roman emperor of Jesus' time. But as a term, even used ironically, it's still very hard to imagine its meaning beyond a male-centred, patriarchal world . . . We've opted for the term, "kin-dom", used by some feminist theologians [and coined by Ada María Isasi-Díaz in her book *Mujerista Theology*], to retain the subversive sense of Jesus' term, but within an expansive idea of how we – human and other-than-human creatures – might discover transformed ways of relating to each other as "kin"' (p. 5).

2 Jewish biblical scholar Amy-Jill Levine reviews the negative connotations of yeast or 'leaven' (particularly in Paul's epistles), but reminds us that there was nothing essentially 'impure' about yeast for first-century Jews. Amy-Jill Levine, *Short Stories by Jesus: The Enigmatic Parables of a Controversial Rabbi* (New York: HarperOne, 2015), pp. 121–30.

3 Pliny the Elder, quoted in James W. Perkinson, *Political Spirituality in an Age of Eco-Apocalypse: Communication and Struggle Across Species, Cultures, and Religions* (New York: Palgrave Macmillan, 2015), pp. 59–60.

4 Perkinson, *Political Spirituality*, pp. 61–5.

5 The Five Marks of Mission were developed by the Anglican Communion and later adopted by the Church of England. They are sometimes summarized by 'five Ts': Tell, Teach, Tend, Transform, Treasure. See 'Marks of Mission', Anglian Communion, <www.anglicancommunion.org/mission/marks-of-mission> (accessed 10 November 2022).

6 A phrase used by (among others) the theologian John Calvin, the artist Marcel Duchamp and the proponent of Asset-Based Community Development, Cormac Russell.

2 Wythenshawe: The Garden City of God

1 John Atherton, *Marginalization* (London: SCM Press, 2003). 'The Double Whammy' is the title of chatper 4.

2 The Five Marks of Mission, as noted in the previous chapter, have been very influential on the mission action planning for the Wythenshawe Team churches. The 'five Ts' of the Marks of Mission – Tell, Teach, Tend, Transform, Treasure – have an accessibility and breadth that resonated with the ministry and mission of the Wythenshawe parishes in their local context, <www.anglicancommunion.org/mission/marks-of-mission> (accessed 10 November 2022).

3 William Temple, *Christianity and Social Order* (London: SCM Press, 1942), p. 73.

4 See Raymond Williams, 'Culture is Ordinary' (1958) in Jim McGuigan (ed.), *Raymond Williams on Culture and Society* (London: Sage Publications, 2014).

5 Temple, *Christianity and Social Order*, p. 69.

6 Temple, *Christianity and Social Order*, p. 58.

7 See James Hawkey, 'Excavating Apostolicity: Christian Communities and Secular Cultures', *Ecumenical Review* 62.3, October 2010, pp. 270–81.

8 *The Church: Towards a Common Vision*, Faith and Order Paper No. 214 (WCC Publications, 2013) II: C, p. 15.

9 The use of the word 'church' was not defined in our project. However, the answers suggest that the local congregations and parish churches were seen as the focus of this question.

10 Interestingly, two very specific needs were identified. One being the importance of the church as a place of music, the other being somewhere to 'bury the neighbour'. This latter reason was the answer from someone who had responded with 'nothing' to the question of what was good in this place.

3 Twydall: From here to the church

1 John Webster, 'On Evangelical Ecclesiology', in *Confessing God: Essays in Christian Dogmatics* (London: T&T Clark, 2005), p. 168.

2 *Lumen gentium*, §8, in Norman P. Tanner (ed.), *Decrees of the Ecumenical Councils*, Vol. 2, *Trent to Vatican II* (Washington: Georgetown University Press, 1990).

3 Brian Brock and Bernd Wannenwetsch, *The Therapy of the Christian Body: A Theological Exposition of Paul's First Letter to the Corinthians*, Vol. 2 (Eugene: Cascade, 2018), pp. 54–5.

4 See 1 Corinthians 1.13.

5 Dietrich Bonhoeffer, *Sanctorum Communio: A Theological Study of the Sociology of the Church*, DBWE vol. 1, edited by Clifford J. Green (Minneapolis: Fortress, 1998), p. 187.

6 It is striking that, unlike in so many similar places throughout the country, Rochester Diocese still resources Twydall with great generosity. Though the congregation is small, and the capacity of the Twydall community to pay for ministry is limited by its vulnerable finances, there has always been a full-time incumbent there. The practical contribution of resources and well-communicated appreciation from bishops, archdeacons and senior diocesan staff of the value and beauty of the church in Twydall contributes a great deal to the parish's self-confidence, to its understanding of its place within the wider diocesan family and also to its generosity of prayer and joy in God's good presence.

7 Willie James Jennings, *Acts* (Louisville: Westminster John Knox, 2017), p. 12.

8 'To each is given the manifestation of the Spirit for the common good' (1 Cor. 12.7).

4 Rubery: Borders and boundaries

1 Elizabeth Ellsworth, *Places of Learning: Media, Architecture, Pedagogy* (Abingdon: Routledge, 2005), pp. 61–2.

2 Annie Gouk and James Rodger, 'The Birmingham Neighbourhoods Where Kids Are Most Affected by Deprivation', Birmingham Live, 14 November 2019, <www.birminghammail.co.uk/news/midlands -news/birmingham-neighbourhoods-kids-most-affected-17252885> (accessed 11 November 2022).

3 Ellsworth, *Places of Learning*, p. 59.

4 David Tracy, *Blessed Rage for Order* (New York: Harper and Row, 1975, reprinted 1988), pp. 92–3.

5 Nicolas Bourriaud, *Relational Aesthetics* (Dijon: Les Presses du Reel, 1998; English translation, 2002), p. 107.

6 Gordon W. Lathrop, *Holy Things: A Liturgical Theology* (Minneapolis: Fortress Press, 1993); Gordon W. Lathrop, *Holy People: A Liturgical Ecclesiology* (Minneapolis: Fortress Press, 1999); Gordon W. Lathrop, *Holy Ground: A Liturgical Cosmology* (Minneapolis: Fortress Press, 2003).

7 Benjamin Gordon-Taylor and Simon Jones, *Celebrating the Eucharist* (London: SPCK, 2005).

8 Robert W. Hovda, *Strong, Loving and Wise: Presiding in Liturgy* (Minnesota: The Liturgical Press, 1976).

9 Lathrop, *Holy People*, p. 21.

10 Paul Tillich, *Dynamics of Faith* (New York: Harper, 1957), pp. 52–4.

11 Lathrop, *Holy Things*, p. 27.

12 Tracy, *Blessed Rage for Order*, p. 162.

13 Michael Perham, *Lively Sacrifice: The Eucharist in the Church of England Today* (London: SPCK, 1992), pp. 15–16.

14 Cláudio Carvalhaes, *What's Worship Got to Do with It? Interpreting Life Liturgically* (Oregon: Cascade Books, 2018).

15 Carvalhaes, *What's Worship Got to Do with It?*, p. 9.

16 Carvalhaes, *What's Worship Got to Do with It?*, p. 10.

17 Carvalhaes, *What's Worship Got to Do with It?*, p. 12.

18 Gordon W. Lathrop, 'Strong Centre, Open Door: A Vision of Continuing Liturgical Renewal', *Worship*, 75:1 (2001), pp. 35–45, **43**.

19 Gordon W. Lathrop, 'Ordo and Coyote: Further Reflections on Order, Disorder and Meaning in Christian Worship', *Worship*, 80:3 (2006), 194–212, p. 195.

20 Lathrop, 'Ordo and Coyote', p. 199.

21 Susan Beaumont, *How to Lead When You Don't Know Where You're Going: Leading in a Liminal Season*, (Washington: Rowman and Littlefield, 2019), p. 2.

22 Beaumont, *How to Lead*, p. 4.

23 Beaumont, *How to Lead*, p. 2.

24 Gordon W. Lathrop, 'Worship in the Twenty-first Century: Contextually Relevant and Catholic', *Currents in Theology and Mission*, 26:4 (1999): 283–313, p. 290.

25 Lathrop, 'Worship in the Twenty-first Century', p. 297.

26 In Donald Hilton, *Liturgy of Life* (London: National Christian Education Council, 1991), adapted from an ordination prayer from the Methodist Church of Singapore.

5 Eltham: The limits of being Christian

1 'The poor of Christ are the Church's special treasure, and the Gospel is their special property . . . the poor are the wealth, the dowry of the Church; they have a sacred character about them; they bring a blessing with them; for they are what Christ, for our sake, made of himself.' Quoted in Michael Ipgrave, 'Poverty and Inequality: Some Questions' (London: Contextual Theology Centre, Dec 2011), <www.theology-centre.org.uk/wp-content/uploads/2013/04/windsor-consultation-ipgrave.pdf> (accessed 11 November 2022), p. 5.

2 Gustavo Gutiérrez, *We Drink from Our Own Wells: The Spiritual Journey of a People*, 20th anniversary ed. (Maryknoll: Orbis Books, 2003), foreword.

3 Royal Borough of Greenwich Ward Profiles, 2011.

4 Martin E. P. Seligman, *Helplessness : On Depression, Development, and Death*, A Series of Books in Psychology (San Francisco, New York: W. H. Freeman; trade distributor, Scribner, 1975).

5 John Bowlby, *Attachment and Loss*, 3 vols. (New York: Basic Books, 1969).

6 Luke 19.1–10; 5.27–29.

7 Richard Bauckham, *Bible and Mission: Christian Witness in a Postmodern World* (Grand Rapids: Baker Academic, 2003).

8 Walter Brueggemann, *The Prophetic Imagination*, second edition (Minneapolis: Fortress Press, 2001).

9 Acts 9.2. The disciples were first called 'Christians' in Acts 11.26, with the growth of the Church in Antioch.

6 Durrington: The place of beauty

1 'Durrington: St Symphorian' parish data, Church Urban Fund, <cuf.org.uk/parish/100127> (accessed 23 November 2022).

2 Gerard Manley Hopkins (1844–89), 'God's Grandeur' (public domain).

3 John Keats (1795–1821), 'Ode on a Grecian Urn' (public domain).

4 Venantius Fortunatus, *Vexilla Regis Prodeunt* v. 4, tr. J. M. Neale (public domain).

5 See 'Work and Labour in Modern European Thought', in Matthew Bullimore (ed.) *Graced Life: The Writings of John Hughes* (London: SCM Press, 2016), p. 75.

6 Cited in a conversation Jamie Hawkey had with Rabbi Helen Freeman.

7 Douglas Hedley, *The Iconic Imagination* (New York, London: Bloomsbury, 2016), p. 254.

8 Hopkins, 'God's Grandeur'.

9 Hopkins, 'God's Grandeur'.

10 I am grateful to Dr Elizabeth Powell, who was initially involved in this project, for this reference.

11 Olivier Clément, *On Human Being: A Spiritual Anthropology* (London: New City, 2000), p. 21.

7 Listening for good news: Reflections on the process

1 See, for example, Reni Eddo-Lodge, *Why I'm No Longer Talking to White People about Race* (London: Bloomsbury, 2017), p. 191.

2 Lynsey Hanley, *Estates: An Intimate History* (London: Granta Books, 2007), pp. 148ff.

Notes

3 See, for example, Al Barrett and Ruth Harley, *Being Interrupted: Reimagining the Church's Mission from the Outside, In* (London: SCM Press, 2020), pp. 37ff.

4 Bishop Philip North, Estates Theology Project proposal document, 2017.

5 North, Estates Theology Project proposal document.

6 Otto Scharmer, *The Essentials of Theory U: Core Principles and Applications* (New York: Berrett-Koehler, 2018).

7 For a nuanced exploration of a theology of witness, see Faith and Order Commission of the Church of England, *Witness* (London: Church House Publishing, 2020).

8 A slogan originally coined by justice movements of disabled people.

9 See the Poverty Truth Commission's website: <poverty-truth.org.uk> (accessed 14 November 2022).

10 Laurie Green, *Let's Do Theology: Resources for Contextual Theology*, second edition (London: Mowbray, 2009).